HOW TO TALK
ABOUT IMMIGRATION

Sunder Katwala, Steve Ballinger
and Matthew Rhodes

BRITISH FUTURE

PUBLISHED BY
British Future
Kean house
6 Kean Street
London WC2B 4AS

AUTHORS
Sunder Katwala, Steve Ballinger and Matthew Rhodes

EDITOR
Steve Ballinger

Design by Soapbox Design
Printed by Smith and Watts Ltd

ABOUT BRITISH FUTURE:
British Future is an independent, non-partisan thinktank engaging people's hopes and fears about integration and migration, opportunity and identity, so that we share a confident and welcoming Britain, inclusive and fair to all.

www.britishfuture.org
Tel. +44 (0) 20 7632 9069
Twitter: @BritishFuture

CONTENTS

ACKNOWLEDGEMENTS

This pamphlet represents the culmination of three years' work from British Future, focused on understanding public attitudes to immigration and the issues that inform the immigration debate – integration, identity and opportunity. In that time we have particularly focused on the attitudes and concerns of those who feel anxious about immigration and the pace of change in modern Britain.

How to talk about immigration shows that the public has far more nuanced views on immigration than is reflected in the current polarised political debate. It suggests that the majority of people would be open to a sensible debate on immigration that excludes racism and prejudice. It examines what people want to talk about and *how* these discussions can be addressed by politicians of both left and right without alienating significant sections of the public.

The pamphlet aims to set out our understanding and analysis of public attitudes to these core topics; to pitch what we hope are new and interesting ideas into the debate for further discussion; and to offer our vision of what an approach to immigration that is principled, practicable and capable of securing public support might look and sound like.

There are many individuals and organisations whose expertise has informed our work and without whom this pamphlet could not have been written.

The authors also wish to thank British Future staff members Joe Cryer and Elizabeth Gibson; former staff members Rachael Jolley, Angie Starn and Helena Stroud; and former interns Binita Mehta, Doug Jefferson and Henry Hill.

We would also like to acknowledge the continuing support and guidance from our trustees: Shirley Cramer (Chair), Wilf Weeks, Howard Jackson, Samira Ahmed, Elizabeth Berridge, Ian Birrell, David Isaac, Alasdair Murray, Shamit Saggar and Ayesha Saran; and former trustees Enver Solomon and David Farnsworth. Also the foundations and trusts that made the launch of British Future possible: Barrow Cadbury Trust, Unbound Philanthropy, Trust for London, Oak Foundation, and Open Society Foundation. We look forward to working with them and with new partners in the years ahead. We are also grateful for the support of the Diana Princess of Wales Memorial Trust during our start-up phase.

Particular thanks to Deborah Mattinson and her colleagues at Britain Thinks, who held deliberative research groups for British Future around the UK: on the economics of immigration in Bolton, Cheltenham and Coventry; on integration in Leeds and Farnham; on student migration in Bristol, Nottingham and York; on EU migration in Southampton; on asylum and refugee protection in London; and on identity and history in Birmingham; Cardiff, Glasgow and High Wycombe.

Thanks to Lord Ashcroft, both for his own research and for giving us the opportunity to pitch an earlier version of these arguments to a 100-strong audience that he had assembled, alongside Sir Andrew Green of Migration Watch. The audience's feedback and his analysis of this, in *Small Island*, was highly valuable.

Thanks too to ICM, Ipsos-Mori and YouGov for their advice in commissioning attitudes research and polling over this period.

We learnt an enormous amount from Frank Sharry, founder and executive director of America's Voice, and are grateful to him for sharing his insights and experiences from many years' work engaging public audiences on immigration in the United States.

British Future would also like to express our gratitude to all of those who have contributed to and advised on our research and analysis over the last three years.

Particular thanks for their engagement with our work through advice and expertise, conversation, debate and critical challenge to: Sughra Ahmed, Mohammed Amin, Tim Bale, Gavin Barwell, Jason Bergen, Rob Berkeley, Keith Best, Polly Billington, Scott Blinder, Mark Boleat, Zrinka Bralo, Jo Broadwood, Mihir Bose, David Bownes, Jan Brulc, Robert Buckland, George Byczynski, Matt Cavanagh, Anthony Clavane, Douglas Carswell, Damian Collins, Tim Collins, Rosa Crawford, Tim Cross, Jon Cruddas, Peter Cunnane, Rowenna Davis, John Denham, Bobby Duffy, David Edgar, Mark Field, Catherine Fieschi, Tim Finch, Robert Fleming, Don Flynn, Robert Ford, Liam Fox, Richard Gander, David Gardner, Dave Garrett, Fiona Gell, Karisia Gichuke, Maurice Glasman, Alex Glennie, David Goodhart, Paul Goodman, Karisia Gichuke, Ruth Grove-White, Matthew Goodwin, Heather Grabbe, Asim Hafiz, Robert Halfon, Russell Hargrave, Atul Hatwal, Mubin Haq, Taryn Higashi, Mark Hilton, Sunny Hundal, Dilwar Hussain, Margot James, Alan Jenkins, Peter Kellner, Andrew Kelly, Omar Khan, Almir Koldzic, Gina Koutsika, Kwame Kweh-Armeh, Jan Krauss, David Lammy, Stephen Lee, Arten Llazari, Amina Lone, Mark Leonard, Jessica Linton, Sara Llewellin, Nick Lowles, Jahan Mahmood, Alex Massie, Alp Mehmet, Bharat Mehta, Mungo Melvin, Tariq Modood, Sarah Mulley, Awale Olad, Eric Ollerenshaw, Julia Onslow-Cole, Laura Padoan, Tom Papworth, Tim Parritt, Vinay Patel, David Pendleton, James Perrott, Debbie Pippard, Jonathan Portes, Jerome Phelps, Nazek Ramadan, Nick Raynsford, Mary Riddell, Ellen Riotte, Marcus Roberts, Ian Robinson, Barbara Roche, Heather Rolfe, Anthony Rowlands, Roudy Shafie, Alok Sharma, Ryan Shorthouse, Julie Siddiqi, Dan Silver, David Skelton, Ruth Smeath, Matt Smith, Maria Sobolewska, Will Somerville, Vivienne Stern, Andrew Stunnell, Will Straw, Rishi Sunak, Stephen Timms, Owen Tudor, Zoe Tyndall, Robin Wales, Natasha Walter, Sayeeda Warsi, Peter Wilding, Emma Williams, Max Wind-Cowie, Adrian Van Klaveren, Simon Woolley, Maurice Wren and Nadhim Zahawi.

We are grateful to the many different groups and organisations who have co-hosted events with us or invited us to speak on these themes with audiences around the country, including: APPG on European Reform, APPG on Migration, Barrow Cadbury Trust, Battle of Ideas, London, the BBC, including the BBC Free Thinking festival, Gateshead, Bright Blue, Bristol University, Bristol Festival of Ideas, The Centre for Entrepreneurs, The Centre for Equality and Diversity, Chatham House, Counterpoint, The Equality and Diversity Forum, European Council for Foreign Relations, the Imperial War Museum, Living Islam/Islamic Society of Britain, NARIC, National Theatre of Wales, Carriagework Theatre, Leeds, ConservativeHome, European Movement, Fabian Society, GLA, The Guardian, IPPR, Leeds Book Festival, Liberal Democrat Migration Policy Group, Migrant Voice, Migration Foundation, Open Society Foundation, Policy Exchange, Policy Network, Progress, Quilliam Foundation, Scottish Refugee Council, Universities UK, University of Oxford, University of Sussex, British-American Business Immigration Conference, British-Spanish Tertiulias, European Programme for Integration and Migration.

INTRODUCTION – HOW TO TALK ABOUT IMMIGRATION

Immigration is the issue that *everyone* is talking about. Repeated surveys show it is neck-and-neck with the economy as number one issue for the public now, and will be come the general election.

With tabloid headlines raging, populist parties on the rise and mainstream politicians rushing to bring out new, 'tougher' policies, it's widely assumed that this means public opinion is unvaryingly hostile towards immigration – and that the only way to connect with people is by 'getting tough' on immigration. Yet research, from British Future and others, shows this is not the case.

When they talk about immigration the public is moderate, not mad.

Most people aren't desperate to pull up the drawbridge and stop all immigration, nor are they crying out for more of it. Instead they're somewhere in the middle: worried about the impacts on jobs, public services and on the 'Britishness' of our culture; but aware of the benefits to our economy. A clear majority opposes prejudice against migrants who come here to better themselves.

Perhaps unsurprisingly, people would rather keep the immigration that they think is OK: people with skills we need and students who bring more money into our universities and the towns where they live. They're also proud of Britain's tradition of protecting refugees fleeing war and persecution. But they would like less of some other types of immigration, such as unskilled workers or people who would be reliant on state benefits.

They also want to be included in a constructive conversation about how we manage the pressures that rapid change can bring. They would welcome an honest debate about the kinds of immigration that the government can control and those that they can't; and about the costs and benefits to the economy of keeping immigration or closing ourselves off from it.

"Winning back people's trust on immigration is not going to be easy."

Yet voters have been excluded from these decisions about what and who we are as a country. We may have moved past "we're not allowed to talk about immigration", but when we do talk about it, politicians still do not trust the public to say something sensible.

Those trying to defend the benefits of immigration have been wary of engaging with the public at all on the issue, in the belief that opinion is too 'toxic'. When they do, their approach has sometimes been actively harmful to their cause: telling someone 'you're wrong, here are the facts' only alienates them further; suggesting that they're a bit racist if they disagree does not win them over.

Advocates of a 'get tough' approach to immigration have gone in a different direction but for similarly misguided reasons. While migration liberals don't trust the public to talk about immigration without things turning nasty, their opponents don't trust voters to handle the realities of trying to control it in the modern world.

Instead they have offered them a tough target that has not been met and was never likely to be. What this unkept promise has done, like the promises before it from governments of varying stripes, is to undermine public trust even further. It is important this mistake isn't repeated in the debate on EU free movement and the proposed renegotiation of Britain's relationship with Europe.

Winning back people's trust on immigration is not going to be easy. What we suggest in *How to talk about immigration*, however, is that it's not impossible.

Our research suggests that a 'moderate majority' of the public – migration liberals together with those who would like small reductions in immigration but would still welcome economic contributors – could agree on a sensible approach to immigration. This certainly seems more feasible than trying to secure agreement between moderate reductionists who still welcome contributors, and those who would like drastic reductions, closed borders or even repatriation. Put those three round a table and it would not be long before one of them had upended it and walked out.

'Keep your promises' might be an obvious starting point when trying to win back trust – and that means making promises you can keep in the first place. But there's a bit more to it than that. Any successful approach must be principled, workable and capable of winning public support – difficult when it might sometimes feel that the three are mutually exclusive. They're not – but, like anything in politics, it's a question of balances and trade-offs.

Politicians' current message to the electorate, whether it is on immigration levels or our relationship with Europe, is "trust us and we'll sort it out". This no longer carries much weight with a public that has heard a lot being promised and has seen little being delivered. What they should actually be saying is "we trust you to help us sort it out – what have you got to say?"

As it stands, politicians don't trust the public, so the public doesn't trust them. People currently trust a migrant who's been here for fifteen years more than they trust the Home Secretary – or any of the party leaders – on immigration.

The pro-migrant element to this finding is revealing. Yes, it shows that there is serious trust deficit when it comes to the political class and immigration; but also that the debate is not so toxic that they cannot engage with it and start to win trust back.

For politicians, getting involved in this conversation may involve a slight leap of faith, but it's not a leap into the dark. Those that make it will find, from most of Britain, balanced and sensible views and a genuine desire to make it work. Moreover, by showing some trust in the public, they might start to win back a little trust themselves.

1. HOW TO UNDERSTAND THE PUBLIC IF YOU WANT TO TALK TO THEM

Because everyone is talking about immigration, the dominant assumption is that the public must be deeply hostile to it. Whoever talks toughest, therefore, will be most likely to connect with them. This argument comes not only from migration sceptics who claim to own public opinion and 'speak for ordinary people'; it is also accepted by migration liberals who concede public opinion to those who are opposed to immigration.

Our research shows that this is not where the public is on immigration. The assumption of public hostility is a mistaken one.

PRESSURES *AND* BENEFITS
Most of the public is perfectly capable of holding a variety of nuanced positions on immigration. They worry about the pace of change and the impact of large numbers of new arrivals on housing, the availability of jobs and the cultural 'feel' of their local area. Yet at the same time they also recognise the economic benefits for employers of being able to hire the skilled workers that they want; for our universities being able to attract the brightest and best students to study (and pay fees) here; and they also feel pride in Britain's long tradition of protecting refugees.

Academic studies,[1] examining in detail public attitudes to issues around identity, race and immigration, have identified distinct sociological 'tribes' into which the British public can be broadly segmented.

At one end are the 'Rejectionists', the 25 per cent of people who would like significant reductions in immigration, or no immigration at all. This group feels 'left behind' by the rapid changes to modern Britain over the last forty years. They are predominantly older, mainly white and predominantly male. They are more likely to live outside a big city. A larger proportion of this group left school at sixteen and they may now be on a lower wage, retired or seeking work. At the extreme ends of this group, some might support repatriation; a small, significant and worrying minority may hold quite toxic, racist views.

At the other end of the scale are the 'Migration Liberals'. This group is younger, more likely to have gone to university and to live in London or another big city. They feel more positive and more confident about the changes that have taken place in Britain and feel that immigration has been good for the country. Searchlight's *'Fear and Hope'* study sub-divides them into 'Confident Multiculturalists' and 'Mainstream Liberals'; they are also the group that the British Social Attitudes Survey[2] identifies as being happy with current immigration levels. Like the Rejectionists they make up around 25 per cent of the population and, like them, their views sit along a scale: some are happy with immigration as it is now; some would support having fewer immigration controls; and some, at the more extreme end, would rather we had no borders or may even wish to realise John Lennon's plea to 'imagine there's no countries' (which is actually not so 'easy if you try'!).

That leaves roughly half of the British public somewhere in between. We call them the 'Anxious Middle'. This is most of Britain – yet they are not the people who are most often heard in the immigration debate.

25% Migration Liberals	50% Anxious Middle	25% Rejectionists

The Anxious Middle are worried about the pressures brought by large-scale immigration but they understand the benefits too. In our research, they are the 61 per cent of the public who agree that "Immigration brings both pressures and economic benefits, so we should control it and choose the immigration that's in Britain's best economic interests". Twenty-four per cent – our 'rejectionists' – say it's "bad for the economy and we should have as little as possible" while 7 per cent – the most enthusiastic end of the liberals – say it's "good for the economy and we should have as much as possible".

Figure 1: The public remains moderate on immigration and the economy

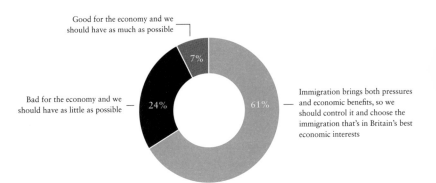

Good for the economy and we should have as much as possible

7%

Bad for the economy and we should have as little as possible

24%

61%

Immigration brings both pressures and economic benefits, so we should control it and choose the immigration that's in Britain's best economic interests

The Anxious Middle are not located in either the 'pro' or the 'anti' camp in the immigration debate. They are up for a sensible conversation about the pressures they feel from immigration and the solutions that might be available.

They don't want to 'pull up the drawbridge' and close the borders. But they don't want to get rid of the borders either.

This analysis is important for advocates on either side of the immigration debate, both those who would like to see less immigration and those keen to defend its benefits. Neither side boasts majority support. Any politician seeking majority approval for their approach to immigration must reach outside their core support, engage the Anxious Middle and convince them that they have an answer. To do so, they will have to engage them in a conversation about their anxieties over the impacts of immigration and what they propose to do about it. All the more reason to try and understand them a bit better.

ECONOMIC VS CULTURAL SCEPTICS
The Anxious Middle, made up of half the country, is not a homogenous group. They come from different backgrounds, live in different places and have different worries. When it comes to their concerns about immigration, however, they can be roughly divided into two groups.

Around half of the Anxious Middle is worried about the economic impact of new arrivals to the country. They don't buy the market-based arguments that immigration is good for the economy as it doesn't seem to be helping them. This kind of pressure is felt most keenly by those on lower incomes or with less secure employment: they worry about the availability of jobs, both for themselves and their children, and about the impact on wages of the "Polish plumber" who undercuts the British competition, or about factories hiring foreign workers because they work for less money.

> *"The Anxious Middle are worried about the pressures brought by large-scale immigration but they understand the benefits too."*

There are some on the liberal left who argue that concern about immigration is all about economics: that when times are tough in the economy, people look to scapegoat 'outsiders'. In fact, the opposite is the case. Ipsos-MORI has tracked levels of public concern about immigration against the health of the economy over several years. They have found that public concern about immigration is lowest when the economy is doing badly (and people are more worried about the economy) and increases as the economy improves (when they worry more about other issues – like immigration).

This is not to say that socio-economic impacts of immigration aren't important to many people – they are. Some 30 per cent of the public, according to Lord Ashcroft's detailed study of attitudes to immigration, *Small Island*,[3] say that they personally have been directly, negatively affected by immigration. Those on lower wages may cite access to social housing, pressure on wages or the availability of jobs; issues like pressure on public services like schools or waiting times in doctors' surgeries may be more widely felt. It is important that these concerns are acknowledged and addressed.

The response most often employed by migration advocates, however, not only fails to address them – it can also aggravate and alienate people further.

> *"It's important to distinguish here between cultural concerns about immigration and racial prejudice."*

These concerns are focused on a very personal understanding of the economy: it is about the amount of money in people's pockets, or the availability of jobs for them and the people they know. Macro-economic messages about the benefits of immigration, using figures in millions or billions of pounds or concerning intangibles like GDP, are unlikely to convince. Telling someone that we are all richer, when they themselves are feeling poorer, is not going to win them over: a more likely reaction will be "bully for you – it's still not working out for me". We examine this in more detail in the next chapter, *How not to talk about immigration: lessons for liberals.*

The other half of this group looks very different. Often in more secure employment, they are less worried about the economic impact of immigration: in fact they may accept the economic argument, that it is good for the economy and provides labour to fill jobs that need doing.

They are deeply concerned, however, about the pace of change in recent years and the cultural impact of immigration on their country. They worry about whether their town still feels 'British' (or, often, 'English') when so many other languages are spoken in the street and in their children's classrooms. And they are worried about whether immigrants share the same "British values" as them. They are more concerned about integration. In particular, as research from Hope Not Hate[4] has shown, they are more likely to be concerned about the integration of Britain's Muslim community.

This cultural scepticism is the stronger of the two factors influencing the Anxious Middle, prevailing over economic concerns.[5]

It's important to distinguish here between cultural concerns about immigration and racial prejudice. They are not the same thing. This was why Gordon Brown's "bigoted woman" comment in 2010, after a doorstep conversation with Labour supporter Gillian Duffy, was such a blunder. In two words the then-PM reinforced the view that the Westminster elite dismisses as prejudice all concerns about immigration.

Britain has a strong cultural commitment to anti-racism. People reject racial prejudice. Voters turned their noses up at the BNP's political offer at the ballot box in the 2014 European election and the party is on its last legs as it slides into bankruptcy, alongside an English Defence League that was disowned by its own founder, Tommy Robinson.

In fact, our research finds that 70 per cent of the Anxious Middle agrees that "increased immigration does have an impact on jobs, public services and the 'Britishness' of our communities. We need to manage that. But let's deal with these issues without being prejudiced and keep racism out of the debate". Just 7 per cent disagree.

The same segmentation of opinion is apparent in people's responses to two polarising statements, offering the extreme ends of the immigration debate:

- 14 per cent agreed with the liberal statement "In an increasingly borderless world, we should welcome anyone who wants to come to Britain and not deter them with border controls."
- 25 per cent agreed with the rejectionist statement "The government should insist that all immigrants should return to the countries they came from, whether they're here legally or illegally."
- 60 per cent of the public didn't support either of these extreme statements. This is the Anxious Middle.

Figure 2: *"In an increasingly borderless world, we should welcome anyone who wants to come to Britain and not deter them with border controls"*

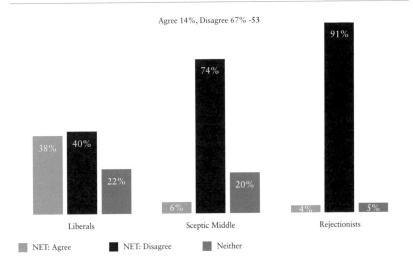

Agree 14%, Disagree 67% -53

Figure 3: *"The government should insist that all immigrants should return to the countries they came from, whether they're here legally or illegally"*

All UK: Agree 25%, Disagree 52%, Net -27%

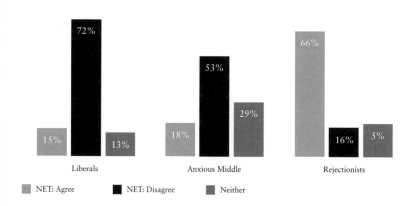

NET: Agree	NET: Disagree	Neither

It is, of course, shocking that a quarter of people agree with the extreme 'send them back' proposition. These views need to be challenged and confronted at grassroots level: there is no gain in trying to appease those who hold such views, as they are unlikely to engage with any immigration proposal that could secure majority support. Yet they are and will remain a minority. While many have concerns about immigration, for most people their issue is with the system, not the migrants.

Foremost among the public's concerns with immigration is having trust in a system that works. People hear big numbers bandied about and images of migrants in Calais trying to jump on board ferries to Britain. They are regularly told that there is a new crackdown – more evidence that it wasn't working before – and then nothing seems to change as a result. They are willing to pay more for a system that works: 77 per cent of the Anxious Middle group agree 'we want an immigration system that is both effective and fair, so we should invest more in border controls'.

They also hear rival politicians quoting different statistics at each other in interviews to prove opposing points. Combined with a widespread belief that the system fails to control or count how many people are coming in and how many are going out, this results in widespread distrust of immigration figures.

A woman in one of our research groups in Coventry summed this up when we asked for responses to the pro-migration argument that immigration brings a 0.5 per cent boost to Britain's GDP: "It can't be true, can it? They don't actually know how many people are here, and how many are here illegally." Another in the same group said "I start to feel sceptical when they start quoting numbers because there's just an element of unreliability about it."

"The public should have a say in the decisions that are made about immigration."

Regaining public trust on immigration should be an imperative for any mainstream politician wishing to engage in the debate. While public opinion is neither irrational nor toxic, public trust is very notably low.

Politicians of all parties have significant work to do in order to win back public trust on immigration. Less than 35 per cent of people say they trust David Cameron (30 per cent), Ed Miliband (27 per cent), Nick Clegg (23 per cent) or Nigel Farage (34 per cent) when they talk about immigration. Home Secretary Theresa May fares no better on 27 per cent. Levels of distrust are all over 50 per cent.

By contrast a migrant who has been here for fifteen years is trusted by a majority of people (51 per cent), more than any politician. Only 28 per cent say they wouldn't trust them when they talk about immigration. Trust increases to 58 per cent if that migrant has gone on to become a British citizen.

Figure 4: *"How much do you trust the following people if or when they talk about immigration?"*

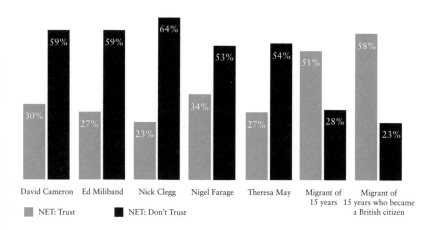

| David Cameron | Ed Miliband | Nick Clegg | Nigel Farage | Theresa May | Migrant of 15 years | Migrant of 15 years who became a British citizen |

▨ NET: Trust ■ NET: Don't Trust

How could politicians restore public trust? Firstly, by engaging the public more in the debate, making clear which aspects of migration they can control and which they can't. They could also set out the costs and benefits of restricting particular flows of immigrants: the government could remove a third of all immigration tomorrow if it stopped international students coming to UK universities, for instance; but doing so would also cost £7 billion and over 130,000 jobs to the economy,[6] dramatically reduce Britain's standing as a world leader in higher education and probably mean some universities would close altogether.

Three-quarters (75 per cent) of people agree that "the public should have a say in the decisions that are made about immigration. We understand that some immigration is needed for the economy and that some is outside the government's control. The government should tell us what they can do, and at what economic cost, so we can make an informed decision about what's best for Britain."

Secondly, trust is secured when politicians make promises they can keep. Trust is undermined when the government sets tough targets and then fails to meet them. But that isn't a reason to abandon targets altogether. Targets can increase trust if they set out what the government intends to do, offering a tangible measure by which it can be held to account by the public.

A target that would help rebuild trust should meet three tests. It should only focus on the migration that is within the government's power to control; it should be concerned with migration that is in our interest to control – and might therefore exclude, for example, the international students that bring money into the economy and are welcomed by the public; and it should be set at a level that can actually be met.

People want the government to get a grip on the system but they are realistic in their expectations. Seventy per cent of people "would rather the government delivered on a realistic target to limit the immigration it can control, rather than a higher target that it may not be able to meet." Just 6 per cent disagree (24 per cent say 'neither' or 'don't know').

Thirdly, trust is restored by paying attention to integration and contribution. Immigration only works when integration works, when people want and are allowed to become 'one of us'. Eighty-three per cent of the public agrees that "To belong to our shared society, everyone must speak our language, obey our laws and pay their taxes – so that everyone who plays by the rules counts as equally British and should be able to reach their potential" (see Figure 12).

Public opinion on immigration is not 'toxic'. The public is more grown-up and able to form sensible opinions than politicians believe. This misperception has led the political elite to distrust voters. And so rather than involving the public in a conversation – about their anxieties and what the potential solutions might be, and the costs and benefits of those solutions – politicians have instead said 'trust us, we will sort this out for you'. And the public does *not* trust them.

Efforts to develop an approach to immigration that is principled, practical and has public support, must start with a conversation. Politicians will have to include in that conversation those outside their core support: without an appeal to the Anxious Middle, neither the Migration Liberals nor the Rejectionists can secure majority support. In the sections that follow, we examine what such an appeal might look like – both in theory and in practice.

SCOTLAND'S MODERATE MAJORITY

Scotland has a more liberal and welcoming public immigration debate. There is a broad political consensus on the benefits of immigration, including to meet future demographic needs. Strongly anti-migration rhetoric lacks legitimacy in Scottish public discourse.

Scottish public attitudes are mildly more pro-immigration, or a little less migration-sceptic, than in England (though not quite so distinctively liberal as the attitudes of Londoners). The differences in public attitudes, however, are less marked than the differences in discourse.

A Migration Observatory study from the University of Oxford[7] found that 58 per cent of Scots would like reduced immigration, compared to three quarters in England and Wales, but more people say that immigration has been good for Scotland (41 per cent) while 31 per cent believe it has had negative consequences.

In ICM polling for British Future, respondents in Scotland (68 per cent) were particularly likely to take the middle ground view that there are both pressures to manage and benefits to be secured from immigration, with 61 per cent saying that across Britain.

There are different demographics and policy perspectives on migration and integration, north and south of the border. Fears of an inexorable decline in Scottish population have now been checked. The Scottish population has stabilised at above five million, a similar level to 1974, while the population of England has increased by ten million during that period.

There have been significant, successful efforts, across the political spectrum, to make clear that Scottishness is civic rather than ethnic. As the Scottish population is 96 per cent white, issues of race and integration have a lower, more localised salience.

The public challenges of managing immigration are different too.

England is a country which is currently experiencing historically high levels of immigration. The core challenge is to secure public consent for how rapid change can be managed effectively and fairly.

Scotland has been a comparatively low migration country, now seeking to gradually attract more migrants to Scotland. If this were to succeed, so that the pace of change were to increase, it would help Scotland to maintain its optimistic and moderate migration discourse and to also pay more attention to constructive ways to manage migration pressures fairly. These might include fairness in the workplace for both migrants and citizens, and promoting an inclusive and welcoming approach to civic integration at the local level.

The Holyrood consensus on the demographic and economic case for increased migration is not yet shared by a public majority: a shift to supplement the facts and figures of the demographic analysis with more efforts to get across the stories of old and new Scots working together would help to popularise the argument for Scotland being a country keen to welcome migrants who come to contribute to its future.

WHAT DOES THE ANXIOUS MIDDLE THINK ABOUT KEY IMMIGRATION ISSUES?

Figure 5: What effect does immigration have on the economy?

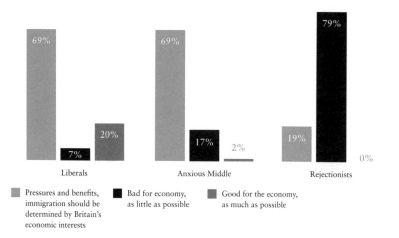

Liberals   Anxious Middle   Rejectionists

■ Pressures and benefits, immigration should be determined by Britain's economic interests

■ Bad for economy, as little as possible

■ Good for the economy, as much as possible

Figure 6: Some migrants come to Britain to work for a few years and then return home; others make their lives here and settle in Britain. When migrants do come to Britain, which of the following options do you think is better?

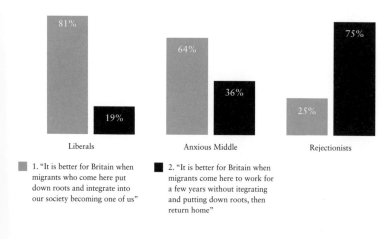

Liberals   Anxious Middle   Rejectionists

■ 1. "It is better for Britain when migrants who come here put down roots and integrate into our society becoming one of us"

■ 2. "It is better for Britain when migrants come here to work for a few years without itegrating and putting down roots, then return home"

Figure 7: *"Immigrants put more into Britain than they take out. Their net contribution is equivalent to more than 4p on the basic rate of income tax, worth £700 per year to someone on an average yearly wage of £26,5000, according to the Organisation for Economic co-operation and Development. This helps fund our public services, cuts the deficit and reduce pressure for deeper cuts or higher tax rises."*

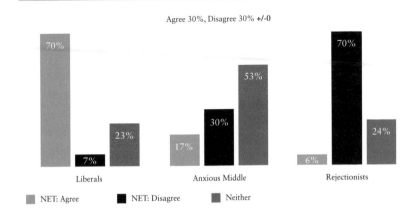

Agree 30%, Disagree 30% +/-0

NET: Agree   NET: Disagree   Neither

2. HOW NOT TO TALK ABOUT IMMIGRATION: LESSONS FOR LIBERALS

Those seeking to defend the positive contributions which immigration can make to British life will be the first to admit that they have yet to win the argument. Public support for reducing immigration remains steady at around 70 per cent and the issue looks set to overtake the economy as the number one topic ahead of the 2015 election.

The idea that there is a way to manage migration fairly, in the interests of citizens and migrants alike, will never appeal to everyone. Yet there is a principled and popular case for it, on which most people could agree.

Those who see immigration as a positive force are a diverse group. They include free-market liberals and multinational companies, as well as their trade bodies like the CBI and the Institute of Directors; university vice-chancellors who want to attract more international students; politicians on the liberal left, supportive of immigration on principled grounds of opposition to discrimination and campaigners for refugee protection and migrants' rights.

Yet whether they make the case for immigration from a position of economic logic or political principle, they have all struggled to make the argument in a way that is persuasive to people who don't already agree with them.

British Future's deliberative research suggests, in fact, that several well-motivated arguments, intended to persuade people who are concerned about immigration, not only fall on deaf ears but can sometimes be actively harmful to the causes they are seeking to promote.

So what's going wrong? And how can those who see immigration as a positive force make their case more persuasively?

I'M SORRY BUT YOU'RE WRONG: THE MYTH OF 'MYTH-BUSTING'

One traditional approach to trying to shift attitudes goes like this: people don't like immigration but many of the things that they believe aren't accurate; if we can just give people the *real facts* then they will be better informed – and so they will stop worrying and realise that migration is a good thing, not a bad thing.

This approach fails – and there is now an extensive research literature that demonstrates this, and helps explain why.

What we could call 'the myth of myth-busting' is not unique to migration. One influential research experiment on health information – testing a typical myth-busting approach listing untrue 'myths' alongside the accurate 'facts' – returned to participants three days later, and found they were more likely to remember and believe the pithy myths, rather than the information explaining they were untrue. The research study concluded that 'The common "facts & myths"format, used in many public information campaigns, runs the risk of spreading misinformation in an attempt to discredit it'.[8]

Myth-busting can be ineffective on many topics, but on immigration even more so – because immigration has a good claim to be the area of public policy where public trust is in shortest supply. When no-one trusts the facts and figures available, an approach that is predicated on facts is unlikely to prove convincing.

Myth-busting exercises are popular with those who are already onside, providing proof that they were right all along and that their opponents were playing fast and loose with the facts. In any contested debate, you will find partisans on both sides enthusiastically retweeting evidence that they were right all along to their fellow supporters, imagining that they are persuading new people too.

The problem is that the undecided are unlikely to have any particular reason to trust one set of factual claims over another. An undecided voter, having watched the EU debate between Nick Clegg and Nigel Farage, told the Ten O'Clock News why it had left him none the wiser about who to believe: *'Both sides fire a lot of facts and figures at you, which they bandy around. Facts and figures – in the end you believe what you want. They are both as convincing as each other. That's the problem. And you don't know quite – well, I can't make my mind up – which side is being honest with these figures'.*[9]

HOW GIVING PEOPLE THE FACTS CAN HARDEN OPPOSITION

British Future and Britain Thinks conducted several workshops to investigate how people think about the economics of migration. After one workshop in Coventry, where participants were presented mainly with factual evidence about the economic benefits of migration, they left reporting higher levels of anxiety about the issue than they began with.

The argument given the very shortest shrift, across several discussions, was a factual report that, without migration, the budget deficit would be x billions higher by 2062, according to the Office for Budget Responsibility.

That is indeed what the government's independent watchdog reports. But there were many reasons why people didn't believe it. People distrust official statistics, particularly those relating to immigration. They have heard ministers, of different political parties, say that we don't have a system which is fit for purpose. They are aware of illegal immigration and concerned about it. They think governments have failed to get a grip. So why would they believe the numbers which the system produces?

Since people don't think the government collects proper data today on who comes in and who goes out, a projection about the impact in fifty years time is seen as pure guesswork – not to mention irrelevant to the concerns they have right now. "I'll be dead by then", said one participant. Another said they'd wondered whether there was a secret plan for economic recovery, but they 'hadn't realised it would be as daft as this'.

A second group in Cheltenham, while also rejecting messages based on statistical claims, found other arguments about Britain needing to compete in the global economy more persuasive: 'We chose that one because it doesn't have any statistics in it,' said one participant. 'This one is pure opinion – so you can trust that'.

A CONVERSATION – NOT A LECTURE

The problem with trying to 'just give people the facts' is that it offers a textbook example of **how not** to have a conversation. What one person (the migration advocate) believes they are saying is not what the other (the sceptical member of the public) hears.

'It's good for the economy' is often the starting point. Yet this argument fails to hit home with someone who feels that the economy isn't working for them. People understand 'the economy' through their direct experience – jobs, wages and the money in their pocket – rather than through GDP and macroeconomic statistics.

> *"The problem with trying to 'just give people the facts' is that it offers a textbook example of **how not** to have a conversation."*

The myth-busting migration advocate will then appeal to facts: that the root of this disagreement is that the sceptic has been misled or denied the accurate information. At best this is often interpreted as a dismissal of their personal experience as invalid; at worst it is simply interpreted as telling them that they're stupid.

Finally, 'unfortunately, there is a lot of prejudice underpinning this' adds the thought 'you might not be prejudiced yourself – but you could well be being duped by somebody else who is.'

This type of argument is consistently shown to actively repel people who were open to persuasion. That is largely because it offers a lecture, not a conversation.

What most people take away from it is very often 'Well, I can see its working out fine for people like you – and I can see you don't care that it isn't working for me'. That risk is only exacerbated if every public voice making the positive case seems to come from the London professional classes, and their main message – based on this myth-busting approach – seems to be 'I'm sorry but you're wrong'.

Demographically, migrants tend to be younger than the population as a whole, meaning they are more likely to be economically active and less likely to be using public services such as health and social care or pensions. This argument that 'they pay in more than they take out' is widely used by migration liberals. While it is accurate, it still fails to convince the public.

ICM polling shows that only 30 per cent of people agree with the following facts-based economic statement: "Immigrants put more into Britain than they take out. Their net contribution is equivalent to more than 4p on the basic rate of income tax, worth £700 per year to someone on an average yearly wage of £26,500, according to the Organisation for Economic Co-operation and Development. This helps fund our public services, cuts the deficit and reduces the pressure for deeper cuts or higher tax rises." Thirty per cent disagree, with a further 30 per cent saying they neither agree nor disagree.

Figure 8: The public is unconvinced by fact-based arguments that immigrants put more money into Britain than they take out

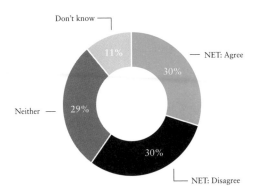

By contrast, the same ICM poll finds that a message based on an appeal to fairness for both British workers and migrants – urging better enforcement of workplace standards so the former aren't undercut and the latter are not exploited – wins the support of two-thirds of the public.

> "While the first of these two messages only appeals to migration liberals who are already onside – and stops there – the second reaches the Anxious Middle too."

Figure 9: How much do you agree or disagree with the following statement: *"Immigration can help fill gaps in the workforce: migrants do the jobs that need doing but which we struggle to fill, like care work and seasonal fruit picking. But for this to work we need to make sure standards like the minimum wage are enforced so British workers aren't undercut and migrant workers aren't exploited"*

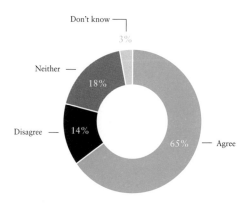

Don't know 3%
Neither 18%
Disagree 14%
Agree 65%

The reason why one message secures only minority support, while the other is persuasive to a majority, can be understood in terms of our 'Anxious Middle' segmentation. While the first of these two messages only appeals to migration liberals who are already onside – and stops there – the second reaches the Anxious Middle too.

FACTS STILL MATTER, BUT...

This is not an argument that facts don't matter. Facts should be important in policy-making.

The job of some public voices – such as civil servants, academics and BBC journalists – is to explain, not to persuade. It is important that the best possible information is available from bodies like the Migration Advisory Committee. It is good for public policy that there is informed public debate and forums that seek to test and scrutinise the arguments from all sides. That can play an important role in keeping advocates on every side of the debate honest, because their reputation in these high-level forums also matters for credibility and influence.

But that is very different from 'just giving people the facts' as a strategy for public engagement or advocacy about immigration.

Ironically, there is an increasingly strong evidence base to demonstrate the failings of evidence-based public advocacy. Professor Drew Westen, a leading US academic and author of *The Political Brain*,[10] has done more than anybody to popularise emerging research findings in political psychology and brain science. Westen notes that liberal advocates 'tend to be intellectual. They like to read and think. They thrive on policy debates, arguments, statistics, and getting the facts right. All that is well and good, but it can be self-destructive politically when allied with a belief in the moral superiority of the cerebral at heart, because moral condescension registers with voters'. This, he suggests, ultimately reflects 'an irrational emotional commitment to rationality – one that renders them, ironically, impervious to both scientific evidence on how the political mind and brain work and to an accurate diagnosis of why their campaigns repeatedly fail'.

There is plenty of scope for evidence-based submissions to policy-makers. When the intention is to engage with general, non-specialist audiences, however, there is no substitute for going and talking to the people with whom these arguments are designed to connect. Those who wish to make a positive case for migration need to do so in a conversation, not a lecture – and they must find out what type of conversation people want to have.

FOUR STEPS TOWARDS A CONVERSATION ABOUT IMMIGRATION

So how might migration liberals try to change the way they talk about immigration in order to do more than preach to the choir? How can they engage with the 'Anxious Middle' of public opinion as well as those already on board?

Step one: stop wishing that we didn't have to talk about immigration

Migration liberals have a fair point when they challenge the idea that people 'aren't allowed to talk about immigration'. It is difficult to identify any period of sustained silence over the last half century. But they harm their own cause if this extends to not wanting to talk about immigration, or to complaining that 'We don't seem to talk about anything else. We've shown that we can talk about immigration, but could you please let me know when we can stop'.

Firstly this implies that they don't have a compelling answer – or that they don't think it's worth engaging those who don't agree with them. Secondly it simply reinforces the 'we're not allowed to talk about it' conspiracy frame. The best way to counter someone saying 'we're not allowed to talk about immigration' is to prove them wrong by talking about it.

Step two: stop looking for the killer fact that will prove that the whole debate is a mistake

No killer fact exists to show that immigration is always good for all people at all times. Even if it did, people may not believe it. And even if everyone agreed on the evidence, differences about values, priorities and preferences would still lead people to disagree on what we should choose to do.

It is true that migrants, overall, make a positive net contribution to GDP. That fact alone, however, doesn't settle which choices should be made about immigration. Some people will argue this shows current migration levels should be maintained or increased. Others would want to be more selective, welcoming more net contributors while deterring others. And some advocates – on both sides – think that there is more to life than GDP: that we should focus more on those who need protection or family reunification; or that slower economic growth is a price worth paying for slowing cultural change.

Step three: acknowledge that there are legitimate anxieties and concerns

Migration liberals repel people that they could engage when they seem to dismiss concerns about immigration as either ill-informed or motivated by prejudice. Doing so risks giving the impression that they don't wish to engage in a conversation with someone who doesn't already agree with their view; or that they dismiss those people's deeply-felt concerns as illegitimate.

Engaging people effectively does *not* mean endorsing mistaken views and misconceptions. But it will usually be more effective to acknowledge what is legitimate and valid about people's concerns – that jobs and opportunities for young people are an important issue, for example, or that there is a need to manage local pressures on housing and school places – rather than appearing to dismiss this by highlighting evidence that it is not linked to migration. That may in turn get a hearing for an approach which addresses the concern constructively: that we should invest, for example, in apprenticeships and opportunities to develop skills here, while also welcoming those with skills we need.

Doing so is not a quick or an easy strategy, but there can be rewards at the end of it. Those seeking policy change on some of the tougher issues for the refugee and asylum sector – such as the detention of asylum seekers or destitution among those refused asylum but unable to return home – will struggle to get a public hearing unless they first engage with concerns about fixing the system.

They may find some interesting parallels in a different debate, which took place on both sides of the Atlantic with very different results, around regularisation of migrants. Campaigners in the US have achieved a two-thirds majority in support of regularisation, through a 'reach the centre' strategy to build a moderate majority coalition. Campaigners in Britain brought together an impressive coalition of their own in 2010 to make a similar proposal. Yet it fell down because of a failure to address the core public issue of mistrust in our ability to control our borders. People thought we would be granting amnesties every other year. The strategy mobilised liberal support very effectively but, without reaching the centre to build a broader coalition, it floundered.

There may also be lessons from the successful campaign to end the detention of child asylum seekers: an emotionally-engaging issue that secured the backing of the Liberal Democrats in government and which the Conservative half of the coalition saw no reason to block.

Step four: bring out the personal everyday lives behind the statistics

There are seven and a half million examples of the everyday contributions which people born abroad are making to British society. Most are neither villains, nor paragons of virtue, just people with the ambition to build a better life for themselves and their families.

While many people are worried about the pace of migration, and want practical steps taken to make migration work fairly, only a minority could accurately be described as anti-migrant. Most anxieties about immigration are tempered by a commitment to fairness – that Britain should welcome those who come to contribute positively.

When British Future asked people – in December 2013, just before Romanian and Bulgarian EU migrants gained the right to work in the UK – what they thought of Polish migrants who had come to Britain, a majority described the Poles as hard-working contributors who don't cause any trouble. In research groups in Southampton, while people expressed fears about new EU migrants coming from Romania, at the same time they spoke warmly about the Poles who were already living in their communities. Numerous academic studies show that increased contact with migrants weakens anti-immigration sentiment in the public.

More people trust a long-term migrant to talk about immigration than they do any of the leading politicians, according to new polling by ICM for British Future. So migrants themselves should be among the most important advocates – not just regarding what migrants can bring to Britain, but also about how we can work together to make migration work fairly for everyone.

According to Migrant Voice, an organisation that aims to project the voices of migrants in the immigration debate, this happens all too infrequently: "The debate on migration takes place largely within the media, yet migrants themselves are all too often subject to a 'code of silence'". Its 2014 report, *Migrants invisible in UK* media, examined the frequency with which migrants are quoted in national media stories about immigration. It concludes "…when migrant voices were included in stories it added greater credibility and more depth to the articles. We recommend media outlets make an effort to interview migrants for stories that affect them or are about them."[11]

HOW TO BRING OUT THE REAL-LIFE STORIES OF CONTRIBUTION AND INTEGRATION – THE REFUGEE JUBILEE STREET PARTY

Coming together, to participate in events that are deeply symbolic of a shared identity, can have a powerful integrative effect, including on the opinions of those who are more sceptical about immigration and integration.

British Future researched audience reactions to 2012 news footage of a Diamond Jubilee street party involving new Britons who came to this country as refugees. A split-sample poll showed that those who saw the film showed a markedly more positive response, with attitudes moving 12–15 per cent on core issues such as whether Britain had developed a confident sense of identity that people could share and whether refugees to Britain were grateful for the opportunities they received.

Interestingly, the film also shifted perceptions positively on issues which were not addressed, such as whether migrants placed a burden on public services.

Step five: unlock the future

If this all sounds very difficult for migration liberals, there is some good news for them too. Demographics are on their side. Young people have more positive views on race, on immigration and on the changes that have happened in modern Britain.[12] Some of the changes to Britain that seem radical to their grandparents will not have seemed like changes at all to them: school classes made up of children from different races and of mixed race, some of whom speak English as a second language, for example.

A challenge for those who wish to secure support for the benefits of immigration, then, is to unlock the future and mobilise the support of the next generation of voters.

Ultimately, how liberals try to make their case will depend on what they hope to achieve.

Anybody who believes that national identity is inherently xenophobic, that borders are an illegitimate constraint on human freedom, or that any acknowledgement of immigration anxieties is simply 'dog whistling', is unlikely to have any viable route to winning those arguments with most of their fellow citizens. They can, of course, seek to build support over time for this more utopian project if they wish. But such views are unusual and niche among most Britons who are positive about immigration, let alone those who aren't.

Migration liberals could find more common ground than they might anticipate with the public as a whole. Most, for example, would agree that the values and motives for treating migrants fairly apply similarly to wanting fair treatment for native British workers too.

One can also acknowledge that the approaches we take to Britain's increasing diversity can make a big difference to whether a diverse society works well or not – while still maintaining that migrant contributions have enriched British culture over the decades.

There may often be public sympathy for individuals trapped and sometimes lost by a dysfunctional system – a refused asylum seeker whose home country is acknowledged to be unsafe, or an ambitious and well-integrated student whose family are being asked to leave – but combined with a belief that we do need rules, and a system that will uphold them fairly and humanely.

The challenge for liberals is to understand that people want a conversation about how we manage migration – not a lecture about why they were wrong. They can still be right on the facts, as long as they realise that engaging people effectively in a conversation about immigration might well involve a bit more give and take than that.

PRO-MIGRATION BUSINESS VOICES NEED TO LEARN A DIFFERENT LANGUAGE

The majority of the British population believes that overall migration damages, rather than helps, economic growth – despite credible economic data showing that overall migration benefits the UK economy.

Perhaps it is not surprising that many still feel that immigration is an economic burden rather than a benefit when headline numbers do not reflect the dynamic impacts of immigration on different sectors, individuals and families.

Many economic arguments made by those favouring a liberal approach and open, flexible labour markets, simply do not connect with the people they are trying to persuade. They may work when discussing the economics of migration with civil servants and expert audiences; but their influence on the broader public opinion that drives much of politics and policy is less effective.

Our own research finds that talk of increased GDP, and other macro-economic data about the positive effect of large-scale migration on economic growth, is often utterly intangible and even alienating to the wider public. In fact, after hearing some of these dry economic arguments we have found that mainstream audiences are sometimes more, not less concerned about immigration! Aggregate statistics aren't helpful and can actually be harmful, because they do not reflect people's real lives – which are not lived in the aggregate.

The task for "pro-migration" liberals is to understand that they must think and sound different if they want to connect with people who live their lives outside of the boardroom or lecture theatre. They need arguments that connect with people who feel anxious about the economic effects of immigration on themselves, their families, their jobs and their towns and cities. It's great to have good economic arguments, but they need to be communicated to people who aren't economists.

Our research finds that public opinion is nuanced, for example, when comparing the benefits of skilled and unskilled migration; and that two-thirds of the public will support messages welcoming migrants who come to Britain to contribute – by working hard, paying their taxes and learning English.

Those who want to make an effective case for the economic benefits of migration have little awareness, at present, of arguments that connect with a sceptical public. What should they do to make their interventions in the debate more effective?

- Priority should be given to finding messages on economic contribution that persuade sceptical audiences while mobilising supporters.

- Attention should also be paid to their choice of messengers: suited metropolitans telling people it's all ok, when the felt experience of many people is quite different, looks unlikely to move the conversation forward.

Effective public messages, delivered by well-chosen messengers, have the potential to unlock untapped public support and make a more significant impact on public and political debate.

3. *WHEN TALKING ISN'T ENOUGH:* WHY MIGRATION SCEPTICS STRUGGLE WITH PUBLIC OPINION TOO

Migration sceptics need little help talking about immigration. They know what they have to say and say it as loudly and as often as they can – often while asserting that others would rather they didn't say anything at all.

They offer a clear 'them and us' story about immigration as a problem – about numbers, pressure on resources, discomfort at cultural change. They bemoan the political elites who have let the people down by failing to acknowledge and address the problems, or even by denying them a debate at all. If they are confident of one thing, migration sceptics stake a claim to speak for the people – sure that they are popular tribunes of the 'them and us' case.

Yet the public politics of migration scepticism are rather more difficult than this apparent public confidence might suggest.

Undoubtedly, migration sceptics can make a strong claim to have done much of the running in the immigration debate over the last decade, reframing media debates and influencing political responses too. But they face a new challenge now. Having done much to articulate the problems and pressures, maintaining their influence will depend on being able to meet the next test: staking a credible claim to provide workable answers too.

Being 'allowed' to talk about immigration is one thing. But can migration sceptics show that they have the answers when they're asked what they would do about it?

WHO ARE THE MIGRATION SCEPTICS?

It is important to acknowledge that 'migration sceptic' is a broad-brush term, covering many different varieties and strands. The focus here is on identifying the challenges in both policy and politics for those public advocates who would, overall, propose a **significantly more restrictionist** approach to immigration than that of Theresa May, David Cameron and the current UK government: those for whom, for example, meeting the government's net migration target of 'tens of thousands' would be nowhere near enough.

The most prominent examples include the pressure groups Migration Watch and Population Matters, together with the Balanced Migration Group of parliamentarians. Another strand of migration scepticism has been reflected in the rise of UKIP, a party whose founding mission is to leave the European Union, while increasingly giving at least as much prominence to campaigning on immigration. Labour peer Maurice Glasman, seeking to construct a socially conservative 'blue Labour' political agenda, has advocated a migration scepticism from the left.

This chapter is concerned, however, only with migration sceptic voices which make significant contributions to mainstream political and policy debates. Extreme fringe groups like the BNP or the EDL are, of course, *entirely opposed* to immigration. But their demonstrably toxic reputation with the vast majority of the public will always limit their reach to a small slice of rejectionist opinion.

Here we are interested in the future challenges for the more sceptical end of the mainstream public migration debate, to show why constructing a principled and workable policy agenda – and one which can secure public confidence and support – may not necessarily prove any easier for migration sceptics than it is for migration liberals.

That is because there are three big headaches for migration sceptics: numbers; an effective policy agenda; and the politics of public consent.

THE NUMBERS HEADACHE

The first headache for migration sceptics is numbers. This may seem counter-intuitive: migration sceptics like to talk about numbers, emphasising the scale of migration and the need to reduce it, while their opponents talk about wanting to move beyond a 'numbers game'.

Migration sceptics take a range of different views on what numbers to focus on – whether to target immigration, or net migration, or whether the real issue is the overall size of the population and what the desired level should be. All agree, however, that whatever it is, it should be much lower than at present. Most would regard even reducing net migration to 100,000 as just a down payment on a more ambitious agenda.

> *"Migration sceptics now face a big numbers headache of their own: how could they persuade a government that is missing its current target to set a much tougher one?"*

The pressure group Population Matters changed its name from the "Optimum Population Trust". People, naturally, tended to ask what they thought the optimum population of the UK should be. Their answer – that Britain will remain overpopulated until the population is reduced back down to the level it was in the 1800s of 20 million[13] (from the current level of 64 million) – sounded alarming to most, even if the plan was a gradualist one, aiming to reduce the population by 2.5 per cent every year, through net emigration and reduced birth rates.

Migration Watch have a considerably more moderate goal, aiming not at a drastic reduction in population, but campaigning on the slogan 'no to 70 million'. They have advocated that this requires net migration to be an absolute maximum of 40,000 a year.

The Balanced Migration group expressed their similar, slightly tighter goal very concisely: "*We believe that immigration should be brought down to the level of emigration*".[14] Their aim is for net migration to be zero.

Whichever numbers they focus on, however, migration sceptics now face a big numbers headache of their own: *How could they persuade a government that is missing its current target to set a much tougher one?*

The answer, one would expect, is to be found in their policy solutions. Which brings us on to their second headache.

POLICY – AND WORKABLE SOLUTIONS

Clearly, groups who want much lower levels of migration need a plan setting out how to get there.

This might start with proposals for how a government that wanted net migration close to zero would cut legal migration to help meet that target. It is hard to see what workable and principled policies, which would still retain public support, have not currently been adopted.

The Balanced Migration group acknowledged the challenge when net migration figures reached 212,000 in May 2014, more than double the target of 'tens of thousands'. Their full statement read:

"These new figures illustrate the difficulty of getting immigration down as the British public most certainly want. They also confirm the need for a target as a focus for government policy. Without the target, net migration today would have been much higher. However, no useful target can be achieved without a major increase in resources devoted to defending our borders."[15]

Resources to defend the borders could deal with illegal migration. It is difficult, however, to see how this would help to reduce *legal* migration by 200,000 a year.

This highlights an unusual feature of the immigration debate. If there was a 'Balanced Budget' group of parliamentarians, the first thing they would expect to be asked for would be the plans to achieve their goal: the spending cuts, the tax rises and other policies. There is no good reason why a 'Balanced Migration' group should face different treatment. A useful 'normalisation' of the immigration debate would be for advocates of significant cuts to immigration numbers to routinely be asked 'how?' so that policymakers, politicians and the public could consider the trade-offs involved.

Another big policy gap for migration sceptics is on integration. Lord Ashcroft[16] reported that the 'Anxious Middle' public audience "were frustrated at what they saw as the lack of positive solutions to the problem" from sceptical advocates. Immigration sceptics have talked predominantly about letting fewer people in and said much less about how they would seek to improve the integration of those migrants who are already here. UKIP proposed an immigration moratorium, in effect a ban on settlement and citizenship for five years. Such a policy would be more likely to impede integration than to encourage it.

This unwillingness to address the question of integration puts migration sceptics on the wrong side of public opinion. As our research has found, a majority of the public prefer it when migrants stay and integrate, rather than staying for a short time without integrating, then return home. This is just one aspect of a bigger problem for migration sceptics, however, as we examine below.

EU FREE MOVEMENT AND POST-BREXIT IMMIGRATION POLICY

Any public voice advocating net migration in the range of zero to 50,000 has to propose withdrawal from the EU. It is surprising that groups like Migration Watch and the Balanced Migration Group have resisted this conclusion so far.

The debate about the reform of EU free movement is an important one. It is likely to be at the centre of debates about immigration.

A range of reform ideas are being discussed, from new transitional rules for future EU accession countries to rules on welfare access and stronger cooperation on criminal justice measures. It is possible that the British government will seek to negotiate some kind of ceiling or 'emergency brake', which would apply to unusually large flows, but few serious observers see any prospect of a work permits system being introduced for EU workers.

No plausible renegotiation strategy is being mooted which could possibly deliver levels of net migration in the range of net zero to 50,000, within the next parliament, while Britain remains within the EU.

However, if quitting the EU is a necessary part of such a plan, it is far from clear that it would be a sufficient one. Leaving Europe is only half of an exit strategy. The question of what economic and migration arrangements the UK would need are yet to be answered. As former cabinet minster Owen Paterson told a ConservativeHome/British Future fringe meeting this Autumn,[17] the populations of Australia and Switzerland, the two countries most often held up as examples of tough immigration policy, have a higher proportion of migrants than the UK.

The question of post-Brexit 'renegotiation' – with both the EU and with non-EU countries – will be something that 'out' voices need to answer.

THE THIRD PROBLEM FOR MIGRATION SCEPTICISM IS PUBLIC OPINION

This may seem an unlikely claim, given how confident sceptics are that they speak for the public. Yet public opinion places constraints on the options for sceptics too. While most people support a reduction in immigration numbers, it is less clear that they would continue to support policies that would achieve this when offered a trade-off.

The largest flow of non-EU migrants included in the immigration statistics, for example, is international students. Research by Universities UK and British Future found that six in ten people say the government should not reduce international student numbers, even if it limits their ability to cut immigration numbers overall. Only 22 per cent support a reduction in student numbers.

Asked which types of immigration we should place tougher restrictions on, most say unskilled migration from outside the EU – a category that is already restricted to close to zero – as well as unskilled EU migration, part of a bigger issue about Britain's place in Europe. They also mention illegal immigration, reflecting a widely-held view that we need to fix the system to get more control over Britain's borders.

It would appear to be very difficult to propose a plan to cut net migration to zero without cutting significant amounts of relatively popular immigration. This may explain why migration sceptics have been reluctant to put one forward.

In the real world, reducing the numbers involves a paradox. The only clear way to address public anxiety about immigration levels is by cutting the forms of immigration about which people are not anxious.

The problem, then, looks less like a systematic betrayal of the public by the political class, and more like a public disagreement about what to do.

WHERE NEXT FOR THE MIGRATION SCEPTICS?

Perhaps there will be a fork in the road among migration sceptics.

Some more moderate migration sceptics – who could be termed 'mainstream restrictionists' – may argue that Theresa May and David Cameron have already made all or most of the feasible, real-world policy changes that they can. They might defend an unsuccessful effort to get net migration down a bit, if not close to 100,000. Some in this group also support EU membership, including the principle of free movement, while seeking what the writer David Goodhart calls 'tweaks, qualifications and exemptions'.[18]

> *"Proposing targets and promises that can't be kept is politically unattractive, and more likely to erode public trust than to restore it."*

Migration sceptics who believe that the current government could have cut immigration much more need to tell us how they would do it.

Clearly, leaving the European Union would certainly be a necessary, if insufficient, part of such a plan. But nobody could yet claim to have produced a credible plan for UK migration policy were we to leave the EU, still less any estimate of what levels would be possible. To date, no migration sceptic group has provided anything resembling a credible plan to reduce net migration levels towards zero, or even to hit the missed 100,000 target.

This leaves migration sceptics with a difficult choice. Accepting that levels of immigration will remain high would be an admission of defeat. But proposing targets and promises that can't be kept is politically unattractive, and more likely to erode public trust than to restore it.

'What is the point in a net migration target that the government cannot meet?' a new Migration Watch briefing mused in July 2014. The modest appeal was for a future government to 'retain a net migration target of some kind' to provide a focus for policy, while accepting that 'it may be that the target will have to be refined and relate to just those parts that the government can control, non-EU for example'. That would look like a more sensible way for the government to make promises it can keep.

Experience may be turning migration sceptics into pragmatists. That might require them not only to talk about cutting immigration – but also to join the debate about how we can manage migration to make it work.

4. HOW TO TALK ABOUT IMMIGRATION WITHOUT BEING RACIST

It isn't racist to talk about immigration – as long as you talk about it without being racist.

Should it really be so much more complicated than that?

The relationship between race and immigration has always been a fraught one. We have started to separate debates about immigration from race relations in British society but that process remains incomplete.

There have long been two competing claims about what the central problem is when it comes to race and immigration. For some, it is the problem of not being able to talk openly about immigration without being called racist. For others, it is the problem posed by those seeking to use the immigration debate as a vehicle for prejudice – so that we risk letting racism back in through the back door.

Each of those fears can mobilise its own distinct constituency at opposing poles of the debate. Yet most people do see some validity in each concern. Many think that politicians were too slow to respond to public concerns about the impact of immigration. But they are also pleased that our social norms against racism are considerably stronger than they were thirty or forty years ago.

While it is important to acknowledge that racism certainly still exists in our society, in the Britain of 2014 it should, nevertheless, be increasingly possible to achieve what most people want: an open and honest debate about immigration which does keep racism and prejudice out. Doing so depends on securing a broad consensus on the following common sense points:

- Firstly, that most public concern about immigration isn't racist – but that some of it is, and that it is important to isolate and marginalise those whose motive is to bring toxic and prejudiced views into the debate.
- Secondly, that engaging constructively with legitimate concerns about immigration is an essential foundation for protecting our majority social norms against racism.
- Thirdly, that the way we talk about and manage immigration in the Britain of 2014 should now make sense to Britons of every colour and creed.

If we can do that, we can secure a valuable prize. Being able to effectively separate immigration and race is important not only in order to debate immigration more confidently, but also to ensure that we continue to talk about racism and prejudice, discrimination and opportunity in our diverse society.

RACE AND IMMIGRATION: THE LONG SHADOW

Race used to be much more central to the debate about immigration. When the government first introduced Commonwealth immigration controls, half a century ago, the measures had a racial motive. Rab Butler's memorandum to his cabinet colleagues explained that the measures would be presented as colour-blind though they were "intended to and would in fact operate on coloured people almost exclusively".[19]

Enoch Powell's infamous 1968 rivers of blood speech polarised the immigration debate, helping to keep race central to it for the decades that followed. The claim that mainstream politicians stayed away from immigration is largely mythological, as evidenced by the restrictive legislation passed in 1968, 1971, 1981 and with increasing frequency since. Powell's legacy, however, included the entrenchment of liberal discomfort in engaging with public sentiment on immigration, and discouraged serious conservative engagement with integration, which he declared to be impossible. These were both setbacks for a necessary debate about how to make the reality of our multi-ethnic society work.[20]

Conservative MEP Daniel Hannan has described this historical legacy of race and immigration well. People were too sceptical, he argues, about the possibility of having a rational and non-racist debate about immigration, but he acknowledges that there were two sides to that story. *'There was a reason people thought this way. They were reacting against hard, brutal racism of a kind that has become mercifully rare: fellow citizens being denied jobs for which they were qualified, turned away as tenants, called foul names, even physically attacked. These things still happen, of course, but their rarity now makes them shocking. The casual racism of the 1970s and early 1980s is today almost unthinkable.'*[21]

It was only perhaps the large-scale Eastern European and Polish migration after 2004 – the largest migration flow in British history and one of white, Christian Europeans – which finally helped to put more distance between immigration and race. Yet the debate about the extent to which views on race drive attitudes towards immigration remains contested. What does the evidence show?

HOW FAR DOES RACISM DRIVE IMMIGRATION ATTITUDES TODAY?

There is a broad consensus that Britain is a significantly less racist society today, a view also held by most ethnic minority Britons.[22] In 1993, 44 per cent of Britons said they would be uncomfortable were their children to marry across ethnic lines. Today, inter-ethnic marriage concerns just 15 per cent of Britons, falling to just 5 per cent of those under 24. The attitudes data shows an especially sharp collapse in levels of prejudice across the generations.

That does not mean racism has disappeared. The racist rump that overtly supports prejudice may be an ageing and shrinking group, but it remains a sizeable minority. One in ten of our fellow citizens expresses support for biological racism and different levels of intelligence between the races, and still denies that non-white Britons can be equally British. As we have seen, a broader group can be fairly described as holding xenophobic and anti-migrant views. That such a sizeable minority – up to one in four people – take a 'shut the border' view, even extending to 'send them all back', shows there is more work needed to tackle and challenge prejudiced views. But these views do not represent what most people think.

> *"Overall, a majority of Britons could fairly be described as having "pro-migrant" views."*

The British Social Attitudes survey[23] ran a split sample experiment so that different respondents were asked about migrants from different backgrounds. Sixty-three per cent said that professional migrants from countries like Poland coming to fill jobs was good for Britain. Twenty-four per cent said they were bad for Britain (a 'net positive' score of +39%). For 'professional migrants from Muslim countries like Pakistan', people thought they were good for Britain by 61 per cent to 22 per cent (also net positive +39 per cent). Most people felt that *unskilled* migrants, whether they came from Eastern Europe or from Pakistan, were bad for Britain. On student immigration, there were clear majorities for welcoming students with good grades, whether from East Asia, Western Europe, Eastern Europe or from Pakistan. Students from all of these backgrounds 'with bad grades' were seen as bad for Britain by 70–75 per cent of respondents.

We can see that most Britons take a broadly colour-blind, pragmatic approach to economic and student migration, where skills and capabilities trump ethnic or cultural background, though the same research found that cultural preferences play more of a role in views about family reunion. Overall, a majority of Britons could fairly be described as having "pro-migrant" views. They hold concerns about the scale and pace of migration but are positive about migrants themselves, actively welcoming those who contribute positively, and are committed to keeping prejudice out of the immigration debate.

The moderate majority in Britain today holds liberal views on race, and rejects the views of a prejudiced minority. Academic Rob Ford, who leads the British Social Attitudes research module on immigration,[24] says:

'There is certainly some racism and prejudice in the immigration debate, but it simply does not fit the evidence to claim that most concern about immigration is rooted in prejudice.' This is not to say that racism, and racists, have been consigned to our history. They have not, and there remains a need for vigilance and a need to challenge those who express racist views. It is also about more than just words: prejudice can and does exist in unvoiced forms, such as discrimination by employers. Structural discrimination needs more attention – it is, however, beyond the scope of this pamphlet, which is primarily concerned with immigration discourse.

HOW TO PROTECT ANTI-PREJUDICE NORMS: WHY MAJORITY SUPPORT MATTERS

There is good evidence that the median citizen, in the Britain of 2014, is a pretty decent judge of what constitutes racism and prejudice. So an important core test can be set: those who want to challenge examples of racism and prejudice should be able to take most people with them. An argument which appeals only to a liberal niche cannot be said to be successfully protecting a broad social norm. This is important: entrenching anti-racism and anti-prejudice norms, so that racist views are seen by most people as *abnormal* rather than merely niche or disagreeable, is key to ensuring that they are kept out of public discourse.

This is not to argue that nothing can be done without majority support. Norms can shift over time, to cover more behaviours and groups. Anti-prejudice campaigners will want, for example, to highlight the role that subconscious prejudice can play. But it is important to do this by engaging with people, not shouting them down.

Importantly, it does not make sense to 'call out' something as racist when it is not, consensually, seen as racist. Choosing to polarise debates about racism from a minority position will damage anti-prejudice norms if campaigners develop a reputation for making unfounded charges, which close down legitimate and necessary debates. By contrast, anti-prejudice norms are reinforced if reasonable anxieties are engaged and people are offered constructive solutions, especially those that can bring people together.

So, what is a legitimate anxiety? And how can it be differentiated from an attempt to pursue a prejudiced grievance?

Probably the best test of a legitimate anxiety is whether somebody is interested in a constructive solution to address it. Those asking questions like 'are there fair opportunities for people like me?', 'how are we handling the pressures locally?' or 'will Britain still be a shared society, not a segregated one?' are looking for answers. The conversation 'what should we do now?' will engage them. It is of little interest, however, to the tiny minority who are emotionally invested in everything going wrong, to verify their conspiracy and betrayal thesis, and prove that the whole 'experiment' of Britain as a multi-ethnic society was bound to fail.

The debate about UKIP and racism
The 2014 European Election campaign offered a prominent case study of how not to talk about immigration and race, with a noisy and polarised debate about the UKIP campaign.

Initially, UKIP came under heavy fire from critics in the media and other campaigners, with its anti-immigration posters lambasted as 'racist' and the party itself labeled as a 'racist party' or the 'BNP in blazers'.

Attitudes surveys[25] clearly demonstrated that these attacks failed to persuade.

The claim that UKIP has 'racist views and many racist members' did make sense to one in four people (27 per cent). It was popular with those who would never have touched UKIP with a bargepole. It carried little weight, however, with those who might have been thinking about supporting the party. UKIP sympathisers were much more likely to be in the group (26 per cent) who saw such attacks as proof that the party was on the right track – that its more controversial candidates were just saying the things ordinary people think.

The middle-ground opinion was that the party did need to do more to clean up its act – that the party was not racist but "does seem to attract some candidates or supporters with racist, extreme or odd views". Sixty per cent rejected the idea that UKIP's posters were racist, however. People were much more likely to think the media coverage was biased against UKIP (47 per cent) than that the coverage was fair (20 per cent) or that UKIP benefitted from media bias in their favour (13 per cent).

If UKIP was helped more than they were harmed by attacks them from their critics, it suffered more self-inflicted damage from the statements of it's own candidates.

The failure to vet candidates properly led to a constant stream of extreme comments, which damaged the party's reputation. What particularly hurt UKIP were comments by its own leader, Nigel Farage, about Romanian migrants. It was *The Sun*, rather than *The Guardian*, which called him out on it most effectively:

'*It is not racist to worry about the impact of millions of migrants on Britain. It is racist to smear Romanians for being Romanian.*'[26]

This was a good example of how messengers matter too. There was a much broader chorus of criticism, well beyond the 'usual suspects', once Farage did cross the line protecting a majority norm.

There were lessons here for both sides.

Those seeking to challenge xenophobia in UKIP needed to show much more discrimination themselves. It was not credible to try to treat UKIP as a toxic and racist party. A more effective challenge would welcome the fact that Nigel Farage does not want to lead a toxic party – and to make UKIP's willingness to police its boundary against extreme candidates and language an important test of his leadership and credibility.

> *"Those seeking to challenge xenophobia in UKIP needed to show much more discrimination themselves."*

For UKIP, the campaign showed that, instead of just complaining about attacks on the party, they needed to accept the responsibility to clean up their act. The party's new immigration spokesman Steven Woolfe seemed to acknowledge this, in taking up the role in July 2014. "It is important for me that we don't stigmatise or give the impression that we are attacking individual nationalities", he said, arguing that while the party would campaign against EU free movement "we must be accepting of people coming here."[27]

UKIP's first MP, Douglas Carswell, issued a similar challenge to the party in his acceptance speech, saying that "we must be a party for all Britain and all Britons: first and second generation as much as every other".[28] That clearly isn't how ethnic minority voters have seen the party so far, which may explain why its support is 99.4 per cent white.[29]

How far those lessons can be kept in mind during the heat of a general election remains to be seen. But effective challenges to prejudice in the immigration debate should always be clear that it is important to have the debate, without prejudice, while keeping racism out of it.

WHY WE NEED TO TALK ABOUT RACE TOO
There may be one final twist in the tail for our difficulty in separating out how we talk about immigration and race. A consistent feature of British Future's deliberative research, across issues of identity, immigration and integration, is the anxiety that many people now feel about talking about race at all.

It is striking how often, in our mixed research groups, white participants wait for non-white participants to raise more challenging issues around integration, before they feel able to contribute to the discussion.

Very occasionally, people did make prejudiced comments, particularly about Roma migrants, or specific minority groups. Much more common, however, are people looking for common ground, clearly committed to anti-racist norms, yet unsure that they have the vocabulary to talk confidently about how we live together. Is it OK to talk about feeling unsettled about the pace of change? How do you talk about those from a different ethnic or faith group if you want to make a point about the value of bringing people from different backgrounds together?

There is a direct challenge here for migration liberals if they genuinely wish to engage in a conversation with people who do not already agree with them. Those who preface comments about immigration with "I'm not racist, but…" have become a much-derided stereotype among those advocating for the benefits of immigration, with an expectation that this will immediately be followed by evidence of their prejudiced views. Our experience is that most people are quite genuine when they say this. It is an expression of the difficulty with which they are attempting to navigate issues of immigration and race. A better response would be to engage and offer help.

As Drew Westen has said of his research into attitudes to demographic change in the United States, when people feel ambivalence about a topic, it is important to find ways to make sure that people can articulate and address that:

"Avoid avoidance. Talk openly about race and ethnicity because people's better angels are their conscious values."[30]

People are gradually becoming more confident that we can talk openly about immigration. Perhaps, in an increasingly diverse, less-racist-but-anxious Britain, we will have some further work to do if we are all to learn how we can talk about race too.

5. WHY INTEGRATION MATTERS: HOW TO MAKE THE 'NEW US' WORK

Over the last decade it has become increasingly clear that the debates about immigration and integration are quite different. The current immigration debate is largely concerned with migration from within the EU and people who have arrived relatively recently from Eastern Europe; while issues of integration have tended to focus on communities that have long resided in the UK.

They are linked in people's minds all the same. For many of those whose anxiety about immigration is based on its perceived impact on our culture, when they talk about immigration they are referring to the mosque down the road or the young people from different backgrounds in the nearby big city. As often as not, the people they mean were born and bred here.

Integration matters to people's attitudes to immigration because their confidence in how we handle integration now affects how they think we will handle immigration in the future. But people with quite different views on immigration can often find common ground on questions of integration and how we can make it work.

Immigration is the act of moving from one country to another, and so of choosing to join a new society. At the heart of making immigration work is this profoundly important question about identity and belonging: how do people become 'one of us'?

People who come from different starting points on immigration can often find more common ground over integration. It is important that they do: immigration debates are about both economics and identity but, ultimately, cultural questions – about who we are and how we live together – are usually trumps.

What we feel about change is highly subjective. If you find change deeply unsettling, you will always struggle to persuade somebody who embraces change of your point of view, or vice versa. But we should still be able to agree that we do have a joint responsibility to make our shared society work. Only a fringe minority would still now disagree that the diversity of modern Britain is a settled and irreversible fact. Most of us think it is important to identify how our common citizenship should work, if we want a shared society, not a divided, polarised and segregated one.

Integration is partly a question of what we expect from migrants. It concerns their responsibilities and what reciprocal rights they can expect, in return, from the society they join. But integration is not only a question for migrants, or for their children and grandchildren to navigate as first, second or third generation Britons. These have to be debates about what identity and belonging mean for all of us if we are all going to have a voice and a stake in how we make the 'new us' work.

IS THE CLUB OPEN OR CLOSED TO NEW MEMBERS?

Can people become 'us'? How open is our national community to newcomers who might seek to join it? Different countries answer that question in different ways and this has a big impact on how they think about both immigration and integration.

Many people in Japan struggle with the idea that somebody could become Japanese. So the idea of being more open to immigration remains a largely taboo subject, no matter how stark the demographic projections have become. At the other end of the spectrum, countries like Canada and the United States have made an idea of themselves, as 'nations of immigrants', part of their national story. For a long time, continental European societies hoped to insulate the economics of migration from questions of identity and belonging, by giving 'guest workers' the right to work while keeping them outside the national community. But Germany has sought to move decisively away from this *gastarbeiter* model, offering citizenship and valuing integration instead. 'We wanted workers, we got people instead', as the playwright Max Frisch famously put it.

Britain did enable migrants to become British. Indeed, the first post-war migrants who arrived on the Windrush were confident that they were British before they arrived, only to find that some of their fellow citizens weren't quite so sure about that. Over the following decades, the argument – for a civic, rather than ethnic, definition of Britishness – was contested but decisively won.

Yet integration remained historically undervalued on both sides of the migration debate. Pro-migration liberals celebrated cultural diversity, and worried that integration might be code for excessive pressure to assimilate, despite a significant liberal shift in British society. Meanwhile, migration sceptics paid little attention to integration either. Perhaps this reflected their dominant concern to keep the numbers down. Encouraging migrants to stay, settle and contribute may have seemed at odds with that. It was also an unfortunate legacy of Powellism that some of those anxious about migration, who might well have set out why integration mattered, too often put forward a highly pessimistic argument that it was simply impossible.

How to join the club

For many Britons, the concept of citizenship is a bit like membership of a club. To belong, one must abide by its rules. The ideas of fairness and contribution are also central for most people: putting something in before one can take something out. British Future's deliberative research, exploring themes of identity, integration and citizenship, in several locations around the country – including Leeds, Farnham in Surrey and Eltham in South London – found that this informs and underpins a broad civic consensus on what makes integration work. There is close to universal agreement on the essential foundations of integration. Respect for the law, the ability to speak English, and the desire to contribute positively to society are widely seen as pretty self-evident common sense foundations.

Figure 10: Which of the following, if any, would you say are the most important for being British?

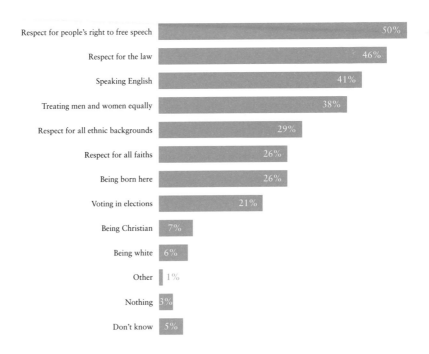

Figure 10: Which of the following, if any, would you say are the most important for being British?

Respect for people's right to free speech	50%
Respect for the law	46%
Speaking English	41%
Treating men and women equally	38%
Respect for all ethnic backgrounds	29%
Respect for all faiths	26%
Being born here	26%
Voting in elections	21%
Being Christian	7%
Being white	6%
Other	1%
Nothing	3%
Don't know	5%

Respect for freedom of speech, even when you disagree, has a good claim to be the foundation stone, and was placed top by the public in an Ipsos-Mori poll for British Future, when asked to identify the most important attributes of being British.

ii) Fairness and reciprocity

Those foundations clearly unlock a broadly held reciprocal commitment to fair treatment: that those who do play by the rules deserve to be treated as members of the British club with equal status.

HOW THE CLUB WELCOMES CONTRIBUTORS AS EQUAL MEMBERS

Contribution and benefits – what people 'put in' to Britain and what they take out – are the public's primary concerns about immigration. Yet there is an equally strong commitment to fairness: that those who do contribute must be accepted as full and equal members of the club.

The British Social Attitudes evidence survey[31] asked respondents how long it should take before migrants have 'full and equal access' to the full range of services and benefits in Britain (which is to set the bar fairly high).

Just 1 per cent say 'never', proposing to permanently shut migrants out of the citizenship and welfare club.

A small proportion believe that a qualifying period for full and equal access should be five years: 25 per cent proposed this as the right approach for non-EU migrants, and just 18 per cent for EU migrants. Most respondents favoured a two to three year period. Clear majorities favoured full and equal access for both non-EU and EU migrants within three years, with 37 per cent believing EU migrants should have full access either immediately or within one year.

Though EU rules make it difficult for government policy to reflect these intuitions, the BSA data does capture the broad and deep public consensus on how citizenship-migration should work. It usually takes five years to become a citizen. There is certainly no public appetite to extend that. Indeed, it is a longer period than most public intuitions would support.

So contribution matters. But the liberal argument, that 'migrants pay more into the pot than they pay out', though it seeks to address this concern about reciprocity, is not the 'slam dunk' answer to immigration concerns that they imagine. That's because 'they are good for us' is still, foundationally, a story of 'them and us', however benignly intended. The idea of net contribution on its own turns out to be a little too transactional and instrumental to resolve the broader issues of identity and belonging which migration also throws up.

iii) Symbols of belonging

The third level of integration is about emotional attachment to British identity, citizenship and symbols of identity. Though this is the most powerful proof of integration, it has also had a lower immediate priority – partly because of an understanding that this will take time to be authentic.

There was also a clear sense of the limits of what could be demanded. British citizens differ over issues like the monarchy or celebrating national saints' days and the same choice must be open to new Britons too. A million British Muslims will wear a Remembrance poppy each November – a powerful symbol of integration – while some British citizens, Muslim and non-Muslim, will choose not to.[32] What is important to citizenship is to know what the symbol means and to make an informed choice as a critical citizen.

In discussion groups on this theme, the idea of personal "choice" was quickly voiced to challenge the idea that people should be judged by whether they watch the same TV programmes and films, or which sporting teams they support.

To some extent, the research suggests that the public would like to ask new Britons to be idealised versions of the selves that they would like to be: patriotic and aware of our history; committed to their families; and hard-working while finding the time to volunteer too.

This links the question of integration of new Britons with the values and norms of citizenship for us all. Holding migrants to a different standard than the rest of us would clearly be unfair. But there is clearly some instrumental value in collective displays of belonging, such as those we saw around the 2012 Olympics and the Jubilee.

STATE OF THE NATION

What is the state of integration in Britain today? It depends where you live and where you look. If integration requires a national sense of the 'new us', it will need to happen locally, where people live, especially as there are quite distinct challenges in different local contexts.

In some places, notably northern mill towns like Blackburn and Oldham, there is now a long-standing, felt sense of entrenched segregration: the 'parallel lives' phenomenon described by Ted Cantle. Here, the challenge is to build or re-establish contact across group lines, in a sustained way, without top-down interventions exacerbating tensions further by creating new grievances. Promoting mixed school intakes is one natural area where we could seek to check and reverse this inheritance of the integration failures of previous generations. Devolving power and budgets to a micro-local level, in a way that requires cooperation across groups, has potential too.

In places where the pace of change has sped up, like Reading or Swindon, economic opportunity is often a key to people feeling that they can rub along together. But ensuring that resources do keep up with population, and that decisions about public services are made in a way that can be understood to be fair, will make a tangible contribution to that, alongside efforts to promote shared experiences that bring people together.

Some of the greatest anxieties are in places of considerably less change such as Norfolk and Grimsby, but where people clearly feel unsettled about diversity elsewhere with which they have little personal contact. Instead of writing-off this anxiety as misplaced or mistaken, it would be better to look at how the identity of the white majority has tended to be neglected in debates about integration and forging an inclusive identity.

Finally, several cities like Bristol and Glasgow, Manchester and London, have found a range of different ways to express a confidence about the role that diversity plays in their distinct civic identities. They offer examples of how a sense of a 'new us' can be fostered, which needs to be now extended and shared more broadly in an era when Britain's diversity is becoming a less urban phenemonon. This should be combined with vigilance about ensuring high diversity areas do not themselves retreat from the mixing, contact and common endeavours that helped them to develop that confidence in the first place.

> *"It is in the nature of integration that the everyday story of people getting along together tends to be invisible."*

It is important that policymakers focus on the challenges and the trouble spots, but this also skews the way that we talk about integration. When integration doesn't work, it sticks out like a sore thumb. But it is in the nature of integration that the everyday story of people getting along together tends to be invisible.

Take the UKIP leader Nigel Farage's claim that "In scores of our cities and market towns, this country, in a short space of time, has, frankly, become unrecognisable". That will have chimed strongly with some people, but a much smaller minority than they might think. Far from an increasing sense that our society is unrecognisable, the last few years have seen people's sense of both national and local belonging increase, as Bobby Duffy of Ipsos-Mori pointed out in a recent Demos report, 'mapping integration':

"Large, robust surveys show levels of belonging to neighbourhoods, local areas and Britain have all increased in recent years. For example, our sense of belonging to our neighbourhoods increased from 70 per cent to 78 per cent between 2003 and 2011 and belonging to Britain increased from 85 per cent to 89 per cent over the same period ...

And it's the same with perceptions of whether people from different backgrounds get on well together and whether people respect ethnic differences. Both of these measures see high levels of agreement, and each have been on the up, with, for example, 86 per cent agreeing that different backgrounds get on well together in 2011, and just about all ethnic groups showing an increase."[33]

If claims of a crisis of identity and belonging don't stack up, there is certainly a broader sense of uncertainty and anxiety.

People think that British values matter. They think it's important that they are taught in schools, by a margin of eight to one. That reflects uncertainty, rather than confidence. Only half of us think that most people have a pretty clear sense of British values, while 43 per cent disagree.[34] Ethnic minority Britons are more confident that most people have a shared sense of British values.

Somehow, we manage to have some highly polarised public debates about integration, even when there is much agreement on the content.

WHAT IS IT THAT CAN BRING US TOGETHER?

Most people agree both that we are a multi-ethnic society now, and that this should mean more attention to the ties that bind us together. To do that, we need to stop seeing integration as a 'minorities' question and realise that if identity matters to minorities, it matters to majorities too.

That means developing an approach to identity which goes beyond 'them and us' to develop a confident and civic approach to identity that we can share. Identity and Britishness need to be taken out of the seminar room and into the real world that people are living in day to day. We won't develop a shared sense of identity by debating the contested concepts of policy experts and academics but by taking practical steps to create contact between people. People need to experience and participate in a confident and shared national identity if they are to truly feel it and believe it.

The commemoration of the centenary of the First World War, for example, will see almost everybody in the country engage with our history. It will come as a surprise to most people that over a million of the soldiers who fought were from empire and commonwealth countries like India and Kenya: that the multi-ethnic and multi-faith armies that fought the war look more like the Britain of 2014 than that of 1914. Our diverse society has more shared history than we think – and engaging with that history, in all of its complexity, helps the classrooms of modern Britain to understand how it shaped the society we are today.

Figure 11: "The British war effort included Empire and Commonwealth soldiers from countries including India and the West Indies, Australia and Canada. It is important for integration today that all of our children are taught about the shared history of a multi-ethnic Britain"

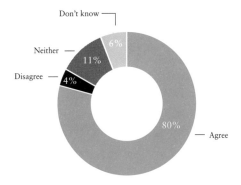

This story of shared contribution and sacrifice needs to be part of the mainstream narrative of the centenary if it is to effectively promote integration, however. Efforts to promote and increase integration need to bring people from different backgrounds and perspectives together on shared ground. At a grassroots level, community cohesion is unlikely to be enhanced by a 'multicultural festival' that attracts only people with predominantly liberal, pro-immigration views. For the English, however, holding a St George's Day parade – *and making sure that everyone is invited and feels welcome* – could be a powerful way to embed a shared sense of identity. A symbolic starting point would be to declare St George's Day a bank holiday.

> "For people in England, Englishness is increasingly a stronger cultural identity than Britishness."

Those who feel angry that they are not allowed to celebrate their Englishness, as well as those who fear that Englishness will be an exclusive, oppositional identity, could all be reassured if greater effort was put into bringing people together on the national saint's day, as already happens to a greater extent in Scotland.

The question of Englishness raises an additional point: that identity and integration debates feel unbalanced if they don't refer to majority identities.[35] For people in England, Englishness is increasingly a stronger cultural identity than Britishness. This has come about gradually over the last decade, as well as being brought into sharper focus through the Scottish independence referendum and the subsequent political challenge of "The English question". Outside of St George's Day, and outside of the football stadium, more attention needs to be paid to Englishness, what it means for people across England and how we can all own and celebrate an inclusive English identity.[36]

IS MUSLIM INTEGRATION DIFFERENT?

'Do British Muslims even want to integrate on similar terms that all of those other faiths thought were a pretty fair deal?' wonders the viewer of the six o'clock news, as it crosses from a row over faith in the Birmingham schools to British-born teenagers heading off to fight in Syria. 'Will Britain ever just accept me for who I am, on equal terms with everyone else?', asks the young British Muslim undergraduate, scanning the tabloid headlines as the latest controversy about halal meat in pizzas hits the front pages.

These difficult conversations are necessary ones for integration and shared citizenship. If questions of Muslim integration are often central to our integration debates, they may feel quite different to the two participants in the above conversation. Both voices might want the answer to be 'yes' – yet they might hear the other voice seeming to say 'no'.

While these debates about the experience of second and third generation Britons are not really about immigration anymore, getting integration right is a crucial 'deal-breaker' issue for cultural sceptics on immigration.

INTEGRATION ANXIETIES

- Most people are conflicted: 63 per cent of Britons believe that 'the vast majority of Muslims are good British citizens', and only 12 per cent disagree; apparently contradicted by just 24 per cent who agree that 'Muslims are compatible with the British way of life' while 48 per cent disagree.[37]
- Fear and anxiety is much more mainstream: 50 per cent believe 'there will be a clash of civilisations between British Muslims and native white Britons' while only 26 per cent disagree. Small minorities predict a clash of civilisations between white Britons and either Hindus (12 per cent), Sikhs (13 per cent) or black Britons (20 per cent).[38]
- Most people believe there is more prejudice against Muslims than other minority groups: 54 per cent of all Britons say that Muslims face 'a lot' of prejudice (and 82 per cent recognise that Muslims do face prejudice); up to 30 per cent now perceive 'a lot' of prejudice

against blacks, Asians or East Europeans; while 1 in 10 believe there is a lot of prejudice against white Britons, with most saying there is 'hardly any'.[39]

- Muslims feel more strongly British than any other faith or ethnic minority: when researchers asked 40,000 households how important being British was to them, every minority household scored more highly than the white population, with Pakistanis topping the list.[40]

- There is confidence about the integration of Muslims. Sixty-seven per cent of people say that the children of British Muslims are integrating well.[41]

The Anxious Middle is certainly very anxious about Muslim integration. And there is an anxious middle among British Muslim citizens too – with similar concerns about jobs and opportunities in Britain today, and worries about the impact on their children's life chances if British Muslims face more prejudice than any other minority.

These findings exemplify Sayeeda Warsi's claim that anti-Muslim discourse can 'pass the dinner table test'[42] in a way that discourse about other minorities would not. They suggest a contrast between a warmth towards fellow citizens who are Muslim – especially if we meet each other as classmates or parents, colleagues and friends – and anxiety about the group, especially likely to be perceived as a monolithic bloc making unreasonable demands by those who have little or no personal contact with British Muslims.

Helping British Muslims to feel as much a part of British society as other ethnic and faith minorities, while getting the worried-but-not-prejudiced members of the mainstream non-Muslim public to a similar place, should be the top priority for those committed to inclusive citizenship and tackling prejudice in British society today.

But that might mean shifting the approach to Muslim integration that we now have.

Firstly, we need to be tough on anti-Muslim prejudice without shutting down legitimate debate
Prejudice against Britain's Muslim community undoubtedly exists and should be challenged. But it should still be possible to debate and critique cultural, political or theological claims that are made by some in the name of Islam, without being prejudiced against Muslims – as long as you keep prejudice out of the debate.

Shutting down reasonable critiques with unfair claims of 'Islamophobia' provides a space within which genuine prejudice can fester; it also reduces the potency of legitimate rebuttal when someone does overstep the mark and express prejudiced views against Muslims. Any successful anti-prejudice strategy should make clear the boundaries between prejudice and legitimate debate.

Secondly, more efforts need to reach the anxious mainstream majority, not just those who are already onside
Efforts to tackle anti-Muslim prejudice should not be directed at those already onside: young people, the better-educated and those who live in bigger cities or who have more personal contact with their Muslim fellow citizens. It is good to entrench that positive shift by engaging the next generation, but the kids are alright.

Anti-prejudice efforts need to reach more anxious audiences: not those with the most toxic anti-Muslim views but those 'moderate majority' citizens who are anxious about Muslim integration while holding benign views of other minorities. Effective anti-prejudice strategies should engage middle Britain and 'middle Muslim Britain' too, including by bringing about new contact between them. A joint jumble sale by the Women's Institute and the local mosque might do more to work out how we live together than any number of post-graduate race relations seminars.

Thirdly, Muslim integration cannot be addressed in isolation; it is fundamentally a question of shared citizenship

While there are distinct challenges relating to Muslim integration and attitudes to British Muslims, tackling the issue in isolation is unlikely to be effective. One commentator responded to Rotherham by calling for a Royal Commission on Muslim integration: that would be precisely the wrong approach. The answer to the challenge of Muslim integration is to define the common ground of *equal and shared citizenship across all groups and individuals in our society.*

There is a clear analogy with debates about Catholic integration, over a much longer period. The IRA bombing campaign during the Troubles undoubtedly impacted on the Irish in Britain in the 1970s and 1980s. In 2014, British Muslims face similar questions. Another group may do so in thirty years time. The question of Muslim integration can not be for Muslims alone: it is up to all of us to find the common ground of shared citizenship that can bring people together.

We should sustain our strong commitment to freedom of religion and belief, combined with respect for the views of others. But there is public concern about those demands that don't seem to be about 'fairness', but which instead seem to "carve out" demands or sound like an attempt to live in a different country within British society. Such demands will undermine the idea of a shared set of rules we all must observe. Faith schools have a legitimate role, as long as they commit to core values of citizenship and cohesion: those requirements must be equally applied across different faith backgrounds.

This broader context matters. It should reassure British Muslims about the dangers of being a special case; and it should reassure the wider British public too.

There is much scope for consensus on integration, an area that has been undervalued in the immigration debate. How we approach integration is a separate issue from choices about who we let in, and in what numbers. Where the two issues converge is at the end result: immigration will only work when integration works too.

Figure 12: *"To belong to our shared society, everyone must speak our language, obey our laws and pay their taxes – so that everyone who plays by the rules counts as equally British, and should be able to reach their potential."*

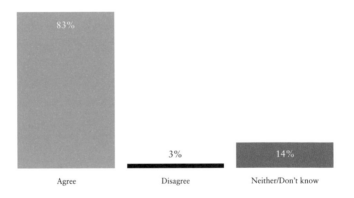

83%		
	3%	14%
Agree	Disagree	Neither/Don't know

"To belong to our shared society, everyone must speak our language, obey our laws and pay their taxes – so that everyone who plays by the rules counts as equally British, and should be able to reach their potential."

In fact the integration deal that we recommend here has particularly broad appeal to the British public, with 83 per cent approval, and just 3 per cent opposition. Strikingly it appeals to 93 per cent of UKIP supporters, with just 3 per cent opposed – as well as to migration liberals and the Anxious Middle.

ICM's new polling for British Future does shed new light on how the public deal with one of the potential trade-offs between immigration and integration. There is a plausible argument that reducing the pace of change, where possible, offers more time and space to get integration right. What people don't favour is an approach that favours short-term migration over settlement and citizenship. People would rather migrants integrated and became 'one of us' than that they merely worked here for a few years and then returned home.

Figure 13: Some migrants come to Britain to work for a few years and then return home; others make their lives here and settle in Britain. When migrants do come to Britain, which of the following options do you think is better?

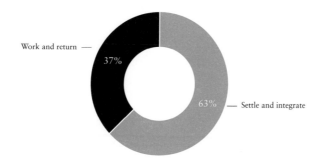

Work and return — 37%

63% — Settle and integrate

The "Gastarbeiter" approach risks failing to turn the short-term challenges of managing immigration into the benefits of integration. Instead, it seems clear that a majority of the public believe that migration works best when we encourage migrants to settle and to become British.

It is when integration works well that Britain benefits most from migration – when people settle here and become invested in the country by starting a family, setting up a businesses and becoming part of their local community. Migration works when migrants and their children get to be fully part of the society that they have joined. What we have sometimes called the benefits of immigration are really the benefits of integration.

6. HOW TO GET THE POLITICS RIGHT: UNLOCKING THE MODERATE MAJORITY FOR MANAGED MIGRATION

Any party that seeks to govern needs an immigration policy that is principled, workable and which can secure public consent. This is challenging – though it is less often noticed how all sides of the migration debate struggle with this trilemma.

Those seeking to defend the economic and cultural benefits of immigration find it difficult to secure consent for historically high levels of migration, or confidence in how it is managed.

Those who would advocate significant further reductions, to bring net migration levels much closer to zero, have failed to identify a workable agenda that could deliver this in the real world. Achieving their target would almost certainly depend on curbing forms of migration that have broad public support.

"The majority of people in Britain have pragmatic and nuanced views – concerned about the scale of immigration, yet welcoming those who contribute positively."

The difficulty in securing public trust leads some to suggest that migration politics is simply an intractable issue. Some business leaders and commentators suggest that immigration policy should be protected from politics and public opinion. That would never be possible. But it is also to misread public opinion. Certainly, the public are sceptical about how immigration is handled, with low trust in how it has been managed by successive governments and little confidence in whether we have a system that works.

Yet the majority of people in Britain have pragmatic and nuanced views – concerned about the scale of immigration, yet welcoming those who contribute positively.

WHY A VIABLE IMMIGRATION POLITICS DEPENDS ON UNLOCKING THE 'MODERATE MAJORITY'

A liberal defence of the economic and cultural benefits of migration will not secure broad majority support if it does not do more to engage public concerns. The liberal minority is growing over time because liberal views are more likely to be held by younger Britons and most of those with university degrees. But liberals need to broaden their appeal, beyond the one-in-four people who are culturally confident about migration, if they want to move on from their current defensive, reactive and ultimately unsuccessful position in seeking to influence the public politics of immigration.

The 'less migration' coalition is much broader but it is inherently unstable, particularly once politicians move from opposition to government. This is because the quarter of the population who favour small but not large reductions in migration have nothing in common, on immigration policy questions, with the one in four whose immigration views are 'shut the border' (and, indeed, 'send them all back').

While those who would like to see a moderate reduction agree with the more hard-line rejectionists on the inadequacy of current responses to managing the pace and pressures of immigration, they *also* agree with migration liberals about many of the positive economic and cultural aspects of migration.

A successful political strategy for those who wish to defend the benefits of migration would therefore be to engage this group in a 'moderate majority' coalition. This could build majority support by combining liberals with moderate reductionists to find effective ways to manage migration. It would also need to engage those who favour larger reductions, where possible, such as those who also share a 'fairness' commitment to welcoming migrants who contribute and integrate.

Such an approach involves some give and take. It would require migration liberals to pay much more attention to three key issues – making the system work effectively, promoting contribution and promoting integration – and to accept the pragmatic reality that there is little practical chance of any significant liberalisation of non-EU migration for the foreseeable future while we remain in the EU.

It would also require moderate reductionists to pay as much attention to 'behind the border' issues, about how we handle migration and the pace of change, as to proposals to reduce numbers. This would still leave significant scope to address key public concerns about having an effective system, about contribution and about integration to make a diverse society work.

In short, nobody is likely to get everything that they want – and those with absolutist positions will certainly be disappointed. This 'moderate majority' approach, however, offers the best shot at a principled, workable and politically viable approach to managing migration in the UK.

Both sides would gain from a moderate majority coalition. For those in the Anxious Middle, who would like to see a moderate reduction in immigration, it would provide a chance to have some of their principal anxieties – about integration and contribution – listened to and addressed. Migration liberals would have a viable means to defend migration that benefits the UK economically or culturally, while upholding our key international humanitarian commitments.

Figure 14: Migration attitudes by party support: *"On a scale of 0–10, has migration had a positive or negative impact on Britain?"* (0 negative, 10 positive)

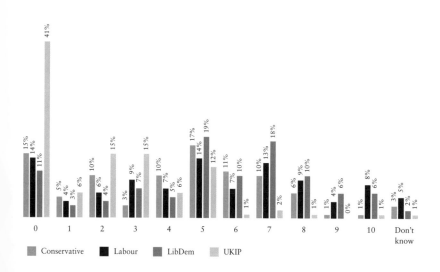

Figure 15: Where is the moderate majority by party?

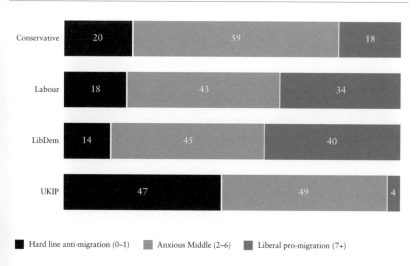

A 'MODERATE MAJORITY' POLITICAL AGENDA TO RESTORE TRUST

An effective agenda would not see immigration as 'good' or 'bad' but would propose a workable agenda to manage the pressures of migration, so as to secure the benefits for Britain.

1. We **are** allowed to talk about immigration – and we should actively do so

It isn't racist to worry about immigration – as long as you keep racism out of the debate. Doing this effectively depends on being clear that legitimate debate about immigration is not being closed down, while a firm line is being taken about prejudice.

Some three or four generations on from Windrush, it is now a settled and irreversible fact that we are a multi-ethnic society. Managing immigration effectively and fairly in the public interest should and does matter to Britons from different ethnic backgrounds. We should be suspicious of approaches that sharply polarise British citizens along racial lines, in whatever direction.

Politicians are showing that they can talk about immigration. A future challenge is how they could practically increase public engagement and give the public more ownership of the trade-offs and choices that policymakers face.

2. Engage anxieties – **don't** dismiss them as irrational, but don't stoke them up either

The New Labour governments were often tone deaf in the way that they engaged (or didn't engage) with public anxieties about immigration. There was an important disconnect between the national level benefits – the advocacy of the net contribution which immigration could make to GDP and the Treasury coffers – and people's lived experience of the pace of change in their local areas. This was particularly evident when East European immigration proved much larger than was anticipated, and so had not been prepared for. The Government was perceived to be dismissing anxieties as irrational and wrong-headed. This only served to reinforce the impression that the university-educated, financially secure and London-based political and business elite had no interest in the anxieties of those who feel less secure.

The current government has seen trust in its migration policy decline sharply over time, despite its efforts to acknowledge and empathise with public concerns. The 'moderate majority' has three main concerns: an immigration system that is fit for purpose; a focus on ensuring that the migrants we choose are those who are willing to contribute; and that we have a shared society, not a segregated one. Practical responses to these issues will resonate – but a headline every week promising a new crackdown is just as likely to send the message that the government doesn't have a grip as to reassure that it does.

WHY A 'GET TOUGH' MESSAGE COULD COST YOU THE ETHNIC MINORITY VOTE

The naïve assumption that ethnic minority voters are pro-immigration – because they or their ancestors were once immigrants themselves – has now turned full circle. It has been replaced by a similarly sweeping misperception that 'get tough' messages on immigration do not turn off ethnic minority voters – that in fact many have similarly sceptical views on immigration as the public as a whole.

As with other public opinion on immigration, the truth is somewhat more nuanced. Ethnic minorities, particularly people born here in the UK, are likely to share the wider public's concern about the impact of immigration on jobs and public services, for example, and on contribution and access to benefits.

Nevertheless, they do remain slightly more pro-immigration as a whole than white Britons.

A third of Britons have a migrant grandparent or parent. And there is clear evidence that those with a family history of migration are considerably more positive about both the economic and cultural impacts of immigration, as the British Social Attitudes survey shows.[43]

Those whose parents were migrants see the economic impacts as positive by 43 per cent to 34 per cent (+9) compared to a net score of +31 for migrants themselves and a net score of – 26 for those whose parents were both British-born. There who have a migrant parent more positive views of the cultural impact on Britain (+17), a view closer to the views of migrants themselves (+36), but contrasting with the anxieties of those with two British-born parents (-17).

The Ethnic Minority British election study also finds more nuanced differences. It finds only mild differences between Asian and white British attitudes to asylum seekers, the survey reports strongly sympathetic attitudes on asylum from mixed-race Britons, Afro-Caribbeans and especially black Africans.

When politicians make cultural arguments about immigration – for example about areas looking 'unrecognisable' or about different languages being spoken on the street – it sends out a very different message: "You thought you were 'one of us' but we don't really think you are".

This is a particular issue for the Conservative Party, which suffers from a significant image problem with minority voters. Conservative support among ethnic minorities is only 16 per cent, compared to 68 per cent for Labour. This holds true despite the fact that many ethnic minority voters hold quite traditionally conservative views on issues like taxation and benefits and the family.

The potential impact for the Tories at the next general election, unless the party extends its appeal among minority voters, is considerable. British Future's 2013 report, From Minority Vote to Majority Challenge,[44] projected that the Conservative Party could have won an additional 500,000 votes – and an outright parliamentary majority – in 2010, if it had appealed to ethnic minority voters to the same extent that it appealed to the electorate as a whole, by increasing its share of the vote among non-white voters from 16 per cent to 37 per cent.

This issue will not go away – in fact it will become more acute. The ethnic minority population in Britain has a younger demographic profile. As the ethnic minority population grows, this "ethnic gap" will punish the Conservative Party more and more at the ballot box.

This demographic profile may offer a way out for Conservatives. Older people from ethnic minorities are less likely to be 'floating voters' and more likely to fixed in their political views. For some these views may include scepticism about the benefits of immigration; but others may display a more tribal attachment to the Labour Party, which for many years has been seen as the natural home for ethnic minority voters. As with the wider population, party affiliation is less fixed among younger voters, particularly graduates. Current voting patterns show a strong preference towards Labour among younger voters; but growing evidence of economic conservatism among young people could offer a chink of light to Tory election strategists.

3. Make promises you can keep – and be clear what you aren't offering too

One important way to get the balance right is to keep the promises that you make – and to refuse to make the promises that you cannot keep.

Promises that appear popular in principle but which cannot be kept in practice will, over time, erode trust rather than rebuild it.

In the current parliament, setting and missing the 'tens of thousands' target for net migration has been a significant factor in a loss of public confidence. It is partly the level at which the target was set; but it is also its scope – any government sets itself up to fail if its targets depend on factors beyond its control, such as EU migration flows and the level of emigration.

Figure 16: *"When politicians talk about immigration, I would be more likely to believe a politician who makes clear the forms of immigration we can currently control and those which we can't"*

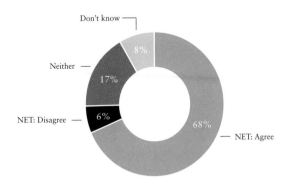

As well as resolving the issue of what migration targets to set next time around, a key issue in the run-up to the 2015 General Election will be what changes the parties say they will seek on EU migration and free movement. Some of the ideas being floated – such as insisting on work permits for EU workers or trying to limit free movement from some members – risk repeating the trap of the net migration target: seeking short-term popularity for an election pledge which would in all likelihood be undeliverable in practice, further undermining public trust.

4. Don't be afraid to disagree – immigration should be a 'normal' issue in politics and policy, not one that is too hot to handle

It is occasionally suggested that the only way to make progress on a heated issue like immigration is to seek a broad cross-party agreement that can take the issue out of politics. Former Labour Home Secretary Charles Clarke's recent book on tough issues, *The Too Difficult Box,*[45] is the latest to suggest that a cross-party consensus "is the only way in which we can eliminate the poisons which have surrounded our national discussions around immigration for so long."

But there is a danger with too much consensus. When one prominent claim is that there is an elite political consensus to lock the public out of the immigration debate, an elite consensus may not be the answer! An effective politics of immigration depends on a public consensus, not an elite one.

"Rather than seeking to remove immigration from the heat of public politics as an exceptional and especially difficult issue, it would be better to try to make it more 'normal'."

This report sets out several areas where those from different political parties and different positions on immigration could find common ground. There is good scope for consensus on making the system work and on the foundations around contribution and integration. But there are plenty of issues – how many visas to make available for particular types of migration, for example – where political and policy disagreement would continue.

Rather than seeking to remove immigration from the heat of public politics as an exceptional and especially difficult issue, it would be better to try to make it more "normal", alongside other major national issues – such as the economy, schools or the NHS – where governments are judged on whether they are achieving what they set out to do and political parties disagree over and debate their specific policy ideas.

The broad principles behind a 'moderate majority' approach to immigration will not settle every policy question. They do, we hope, offer some key pointers as to how to develop public confidence in an effective managed migration system.

In the policy section of this report, we offer a series of policy recommendations that could secure the support of a moderate majority of the British public and help to address some of the issues and anxieties around immigration and integration.

5. Be authentic – offer answers that fit your values

Politicians are mistaken if they believe that they can become popular on immigration simply by saying what they think the public wants to hear. That strategy has been tried and found wanting: public trust has continued to fall, and voters are ever-less likely to believe eye-catching slogans that generate headlines but don't seem to lead to change. That leads to the charge not just of out-of-touch politicians, but of inauthenticity too. So each of the political parties needs to come up with its own voice and its own contribution to how Britain can manage migration, pursuing its political principles and agenda in a way that might take the public with it.

The Labour party has struggled most with how to talk about immigration, having been in charge as migration rose while trust in its handling fell sharply. Most people felt that Labour was too slow to respond to concerns about the pace and pressures of migration, and too quick to dismiss concerns as prejudiced. However, when Labour leaders have sought to respond with tough soundbites like "British jobs for British workers" the Labour Party has sounded inauthentic, risking becoming still more mistrusted.

Labour is a poor substitute for a populist anti-immigration party, but the centre-left party does sound more authentic on immigration when it voices the social democratic reasons to address the pressures of migration, such as by addressing exploitation in the workplace, and being vigilant about impacts on wage inequalities, or discrimination. At the same time, Labour would naturally want to promote the positive contribution of migrants to the NHS, and to job creation in the economy, and for universities and science. The argument that migrants learning English is important for the communities they join, and good for migrants themselves, rings true from Labour voices too.

Labour is considerably more comfortable engaging with the policy dilemmas of managing migration than finding its voice in the public conversation. It is seeking to develop a pragmatic policy agenda, acknowledging pressures and benefits, and proposing a nuanced approach to the different migration flows. But Labour voices also need to recognise why a tendency to jump straight to a policy response can be too narrow. An understanding of migration pressures as only reflecting misplaced concerns about jobs, housing and public services can lead to an instinct to try to 'change the subject', as quickly as possible. Policies in these areas can help to address migration pressures, but Labour voices need to learn to be much more comfortable talking about how people feel about rapid social and cultural change, and to acknowledge how and when that change can feel unsettling, while remaining confident of its ability to challenge prejudice, to tackle discrimination and promote fairness for all groups. The importance of cultural identity in the migration and EU debates – in particular the recognition of Englishness – is still missed by too many Labour voices.

Conservatives are inauthentic on immigration if they blame the sharp-elbowed middle classes for employing migrant labour, or bash business for betraying the workers. The Conservatives aren't credible as an anti-business or anti-growth party, but they do sound like themselves when they praise the initiative and hard work of those who come here to contribute positively, while being strict on welfare dependency, and seeking to promote aspiration and social mobility across British society too. It is natural that Conservatives would worry about the pace of cultural change, and to uphold the value of national identity, the importance of integration across every faith and ethnic group, and the value of community cohesion at a local level. For similar reasons, it would make sense for Conservatives to actively embrace and welcome migrants who express pride in their adopted country, so that New Britons and their children share the inheritance and commitment to upholding British values and traditions, even as the demographics change.

The big Conservative manifesto headache is how to replace its missed target on net migration with a promise that can be kept. A recent high-profile front-page briefing from Downing Street suggested that the manifesto might even simply repeat the failed pledge, by claiming that a successful EU renegotiation could now deliver the 'tens of thousands' level next time around. That would simply be an exercise in denial and a recipe for repeated failure. Such a pledge would quickly fall apart under the most cursory media and political scrutiny, and the public simply wouldn't believe it. If a government were re-elected on that platform, the likely outcome would be for it to become as mistrusted on migration as its Labour predecessor.

> *"The big Conservative manifesto headache is how to replace its missed target with a promise that can be kept."*

Ultimately, the Conservative party's core public pitch is that it is a serious party of grown-up government, capable of taking important, sometimes tough decisions in the national interest. Such a party can never outflank populists with 'party of no' messages: people won't believe that its leading politicians believe what they are saying, nor have plans to back-up the slogans. The Conservatives therefore need to maintain a balanced message and agenda on migration, as David Cameron tried to do in 2010, and not to be pushed away from a moderate majority agenda in pursuit of the most anti-migration minority, who it is unlikely to reach.

Chancellor George Osborne almost never speaks about immigration. This strategic silence means that only half of the rationale for a balanced policy gets heard – the Home Office case for why migration control is important. The need to keep the migration that benefits the economic recovery, which the Treasury thinks necessary too, is rarely made nor heard. The Conservatives risk conceding the public argument to UKIP if they talk exclusively about the problems from migration, and never about the gains from managed migration too.

Liberal Democrats are inauthentic on immigration if they mute their own voice and try not to say anything at all, for fear that the other parties are more likely to be in touch with public attitudes. Liberal Democrats are authentic when they do provide a liberal voice which speaks up for the positive cultural and economic contributions of migration to British life, and could do so more successfully when they acknowledge, as democrats, that they take seriously the political challenges of rebuilding public confidence for managed migration, and handling its pressures, so as to broaden support for the values of Britain being an inclusive, welcoming and fair society.

Given their strong civil liberties commitments, Liberal Democrats, like the Green Party, should certainly remain a clear voice for protecting Britain's core humanitarian obligations, and in pressing for these to be reflected in practice in our immigration system. The 'moderate majority' analysis of this pamphlet suggests that it would be a mistake for the party to measure the purity of its liberal conscience by the unpopularity of the principled and defiantly unpopular positions it can strike. That would risk making liberalism little more than a badge of political differentiation, rather than taking seriously the challenges of building the alliances and support to make liberal change possible – as it successfully did on child detention.

So the Lib Dems should work with civic movements to build support for reform, while constructively challenging its civic allies to help find answers to address the public, political and policy barriers to creating a system that is both effective and humane. Broadening alliances for liberal reform across civic and party boundaries is an important way to maximise the chances of influencing the policy debate in other parties, or making progress if the Lib Dems should find themselves once again negotiating over coalition policies after a future general election.

"Liberal Democrats are inauthentic on immigration if they mute their own voice and try not to say anything at all, for fear that the other parties are more likely to be in touch."

Curiously, though few have yet noticed it, it is UKIP that might yet face the biggest dilemma about its future approach to migration. Campaigning on immigration has been the making of UKIP, yet going too tough on immigration could yet be the breaking of it too. Yet this all depends on a question of authenticity too: what does UKIP think it is ultimately for?

Were UKIP mainly interested in UKIP, its own public profile and share of voice in British politics, then there is a good argument that it shouldn't change much at all. It has found a minority niche in British politics – and it is filling it successfully. UKIP's current 'party of no' messages are pitch perfect for many of the 'left behind' quarter of British society. There are prizes on offer to the purple party for articulating their frustrations and fear of change: victory in the low turnout, European elections; maybe 10 per cent, perhaps even

15 per cent of the General Election vote; a fair shot at half a dozen constituency races in 2015; and maybe a longer-term presence as an insurgent voice of northern opposition. But what that could not do is to get Britain out of the European Union. What is good for UKIP could yet harm the party's founding mission and cause.

A British vote to leave could not be won by voicing the frustrations of the 25 per cent who feel most 'left behind' by immigration, economic and cultural change but requires the support of 50 per cent of voters. If UKIP made a political breakthrough while being perceived as a pessimistic 'party of no' or a voice of 'angry nativism', seeming to reject modern Britain, and failing to offer a positive account of its future outside the European Union, then it will make it impossible for UKIP and its 'Better Off Out' allies to win a referendum on British membership of the EU. This challenge as to how UKIP would need to change to stay true to its founding purpose has been put most clearly by UKIP's first elected MP, Douglas Carswell. The democratic challenge of a referendum means that the populist outsider party has to think just as much about the challenges of reaching Britain's moderate majority as those parties which want to govern.

7. SO WHAT ABOUT EUROPE? THE EU FREE MOVEMENT CONUNDRUM

"Britain, I know you want this sorted so I will go to Brussels, I will not take no for an answer and when it comes to free movement – I will get what Britain needs"
– David Cameron, Birmingham, October 2014

The Prime Minister's pledge to place EU free movement *"at the very heart of my renegotiation strategy for Europe"* confirmed that this is now the most important live question in the politics of both immigration and Britain's place in Europe.

There are four broad positions in the public and political debate about EU free movement – but none of them has yet answered significant questions about the challenge that each faces.

• The strong pro-Europeans: Britain should stay in the EU, free movement is a good thing, and reform is simply impossible or undesirable. This 'status quo' position is a coherent one, but only about one in four Britons supports it.

The unanswered question for Europhiles is how to secure public consent for free movement, and a public mandate for continued British membership of the EU in any future referendum.

• The more moderate 'stay in' view is that free movement is at least a price worth paying for the benefits of club membership, but that reforms to free movement should be possible.

The unanswered question for the negotiators is what reforms might be both desirable and possible – and what the limits of achievable reform are.

- A moderate Eurosceptic position is that there may be some benefits of EU membership, but that EU free movement in a club with 28 members is too high a price to pay. The demand is that Britain should set a 'red line' seeking major treaty changes – such as work permits for EU migrants on a similar basis to non-EU migration – if it is to stay in.

  The unanswered question for the sceptics is what the diplomatic and political strategy looks like that could secure allies for reform on this scale.

- Fourth, strong "outers" argue that it is simply impossible to have any significant change in the free movement rules, and so the only choice is to leave. This is a coherent position, but it does not, so far at least, command majority support, and leaving is only half of an exit policy anyway.

  The unanswered question for the "out" camp is what "out" would look like: what economic and migration deals the UK would have if we did leave.

The Prime Minister's tough language included no specific pledges – nor much detail about what he believes Britain "needs". There may be a tactical case for trying to use strong language while kicking the debate about content into the post-election long grass. But that is unlikely to be sustainable.

When immigration and Europe are the two issues on which political trust are in scarcest supply, attempting to duck the details of renegotiation for a year or two could prove a very risky strategy. It risks turning the EU renegotation into some kind of conjuring trick, as the audience waits expectantly or, for many, considerably more sceptically, to see if the Prime Minister really can pull a rabbit out of the hat.

If no rabbit can be found, the audience won't be impressed to be told that the small print never promised one. This risks repeating the experience of the net migration target, before 2010, when a popular soundbite becomes an unkept promise in office.

Even conjuring up a reasonable, medium-sized rabbit might go down as something of a disappointment, after all of the drum rolls and razzmatazz, if people thought they were promised more than could ever be delivered.

So, unless he really does have a magic wand up his sleeve, the Prime Minister should adopt a more open strategy about the content and challenges of his renegotiation plans.

Instead of asking people to trust him, he should trust them to engage seriously with the choices on offer. His government should produce ideas and proposals; there should be parliamentary debates and committee hearings. He should seek to build a broader coalition for achievable reforms, for example, across the political spectrum and with trade unions, to seek more allies among EU governments.

This could help to open up a public debate about these choices that has seldom gone beyond soundbites and slogans.

The Labour party changed their language, from 'free movement' to 'fair movement', but there has been little evidence of policy measures to accompany the rebrand.

Since it is now talking about 'fair movement', and **will** want to campaign for Britain to remain in the EU, it would make strong sense for the Labour party to explicitly offer bipartisan support to the Prime Minister as he seeks reforms to EU free movement and how to manage EU migration fairly. In doing so, Labour could also champion the opening up of a closed diplomatic negotiation between governments and Brussels, so that it can engage Parliament, British business, trade unions and voices around the country on the nature of the achievable reforms that the UK could seek with its partners. Labour should also offer to practically engage European centre-left parties and trade unions to strengthen the coalition of support for workable reforms to free movement and workplace protections, perhaps by identifying a senior party figure who could make a practical contribution to Downing Street's diplomatic strategy by engaging key centre-left political voices in the EU.

The Conservative debate is complicated by a divide between sincere and insincere renegotiation suggestions. Some voices are looking for practical answers; others may propose 'red lines' that they hope will fail, in order to show that they have exhausted the possibilities, while their real preference is to quit.

The Liberal Democrats have made few significant contributions to the debate about reforming free movement, since they broadly share the view that there is no possibility of change.

But pro-Europeans should be wary of closing down the debate about EU free movement before it has begun. The argument that, if we stay in the club, we need to play by the rules, makes sense to people. But a club where the rules aren't even up for discussion among the members sounds much less attractive. Those who do want to defend and secure consent for free movement should be engaging much more seriously with proposals, short of treaty changes, which could make it work better, particularly at a local level, on challenges like workplace fairness and integration, particularly seeking approaches which protect the interests of both citizens and migrants at the same time.

Those who want more significant reforms need to put together a proper strategy to build political support at home and around the EU.

The thinktank Open Europe has been among the few public voices to offer constructive and detailed analysis of the reform options. Open Europe has itself proposed a series of measures to give national governments greater control over access to welfare, pointing out that these changes would have support from several EU governments and would not require treaty changes but a qualified majority vote among governments and the agreement of the European Parliament.

Demos Director David Goodhart has suggested that a new approach to welfare contribution would be both deliverable in the EU and could secure public consent too.[46] Others, particularly trade unionists, have suggested a focus on fair employment rights.

By contrast, proposals for a points-based system for EU migrants or quotas would be much more difficult to achieve.

It should be possible to secure broad EU support for different transitional controls when new members join the EU. This may provide reassurance to the public. The prospect of Turkish accession is anyway somewhat distant, but it is inconceivable that there would be political support to admit Turkey across the EU using the existing transitional arrangements.

With migration flows from within the current EU, the government has floated the idea of introducing an 'emergency brake' in the event of 'destabilising' levels of migration.

An emergency brake might perhaps be achievable in negotiations, particularly if this was genuinely set at 'emergency' levels. It would be less likely to be negotiable at levels well below current migration flows. The emergency brake idea may, therefore, have little practical impact, though it would be a possible source of reassurance, for example at the time of a new accession, that there could be millions of migrants arriving. But the emergency brake would be a largely symbolic measure, unless there was a more significant economic crisis in the EU.

A more practical policy might be for the UK government to propose a new EU-wide 'Free Movement Impacts Fund', modelled along the lines of the European Globalisation Adjustment Fund (which supports workers to find a new job in the case of large-scale redundancies). A Free Movement Impacts Fund would be divided, each year, in proportion to the flows of EU migrants to each member state. A condition should be that the resources were allocated directly to local level, with national governments expected to use these to support areas of rapid change.

8. MAKING MIGRATION WORK FOR BRITAIN – TEN KEY POLICY CHALLENGES FOR MANAGING MIGRATION FAIRLY

We want and need to **talk** about immigration, because is about much more than the immigration policy choices we make. It is about how our society has changed, how people feel about that and how to make it work. Politicians or parties who rush to engage only with policy responses can risk missing that broader conversation about the state of the nation.

But the policy choices that are made about immigration are important if they can set out an approach to manage the pressures and secure the benefits of migration.

This is a brief survey of the policy issues that the general public are most likely to see as the key tests of a fair managed migration policy, on which we can secure public consent. This is not an attempt to settle every policy question in migration politics: there are a great many more detailed policy areas which need to be addressed in an immigration system. Nor do these proposals seek to settle all contested policy questions: how many visas are made available via a particular route, or what the overall immigration limits should be. This is a framework for deeper public and political scrutiny of those ongoing choices.

The policy responses from any political party, and from every perspective in the migration debate, should be expected to meet these key 'public interest' tests for an effective migration policy.

Competence

How governments implement the choices that our democracy makes, about what forms and levels of immigration are in Britain's interests and reflect our values.

Fairness
Whether we see the pressures *and* the benefits of migration being shared; and whether the system gives everyone – migrant and non-migrant alike – a 'fair shot'.

Identity
Who we are and what we share in a fast-changing society; and how people who join our society get to become "us".

Democracy
Making sure that we do all have a voice in the decisions that are made and a responsibility to contribute to some of the important choices that we face as a society.

What are the approaches to these challenges that could secure broad majority support for how Britain can manage immigration today?

1. Fix the system: invest in an immigration system that is effective, fair and humane

The public lack confidence in how immigration is managed. They have heard governments, led by both major parties, declare that the system is 'not fit for purpose'. They are sceptical about whether anything much has improved, not least because governments have not reached the high-profile goals that they have set for themselves.

So delivering an effective and fair system is an essential foundation for restoring public confidence in how migration is managed. Immigration is the second most significant area of public concern after the economy. Yet we allocate just 0.2 per cent of public spending to our immigration system.

With more than 100 million people crossing our borders each year – for trade and tourism, as well as study, work and settlement – investing in a system that keeps Britain open for business, while having proper controls to manage immigration effectively, is an important national interest.

Our polling shows there is broad public support, across the political spectrum, for investing more in a system that can fairly deliver on whatever political choices are made about immigration policy. Whatever their other policy disagreements, the political parties should find common ground on the importance of resourcing the system adequately to respond to growing demands. Those parts of the Home Office budget dealing with immigration should be ring-fenced in the next parliament. Cooperation on systemic reform would be an important way to seek to break the pattern of major overhauls being introduced and then scrapped as the process of another overhaul is repeated.

"The system for making and enforcing decisions on asylum claims should be reformed to ensure that it is both effective and humane."

The development of the role of the Independent Chief Inspector of Borders and Immigration has been welcome and overdue, as has greater exposure to the Home Affairs Select Committee and various audit bodies. While accountability has improved in recent years, the level of executive rule-making powers on immigration is considerably greater than in other developed countries.

There should be greater parliamentary and public scrutiny of those charged with protecting our borders. Transparency could be increased through the publication of sanctions, enforcement criteria, detailed costings and justifications for resource allocation. This could also include obtaining feedback from people who have been through the system and have been awarded status.

The system for making and enforcing decisions on asylum claims should be reformed to ensure that it is both effective and humane. Poor initial decision-making on asylum claims helps no-one and many decisions are overturned on appeal. It is unfair on those who have a legitimate claim to protection from war and persecution; it leads to costly appeals; and it means the system functions inefficiently, with cases having to be re-heard after lengthy delays.

Proposals from the Centre for Social Justice thinktank,[47] to separate the functions of enforcement, decision-making and support, would increase trust and transparency and should be given serious consideration.

A recently published report from the CentreForum thinktank also looks at the need to reform initial decision-making and addresses the practicalities of how this could be done.

Parliamentarians should take up this debate: joint hearings by the Home Affairs and Justice Select Committees would be a good forum in which to scrutinise the case for reform in the interests of effective and fair decision-making.

2. Set sensible limits to migration and make promises you can keep
There are limits to immigration. The migration targets that a government sets have both a practical importance – defining who can get in and why – and a symbolic one too. They demonstrate that the British government and Parliament decide migration policy.

Britain needs sensible limits. That means debating which migration choices reflect Britain's interests and values, and avoiding making choices that would damage Britain's economy, society or standing in the world. Setting sensible limits also means making promises that can be kept. This means targets should apply to migration flows that the government can control and that it is in Britain's interests to contain or limit.

Since **emigration** levels are not subject to government control or direct policy interventions, any headline annual target should be about immigration, rather than emigration (or net migration), though the government can and should take shifts in emigration levels into account when recommending targets and limits for the next year.

It would be sensible for a government to choose to set an annual target for non-EU immigration as a whole, setting out the policies, controls and selection criteria for component flows of migration within it, and invite much greater political, policy and public scrutiny of these choices.

Migration flows that are not subject to specific numbers targets, such as EU migration and the protection of refugees, should also be scrutinised and debated.

3. Increase democratic accountability and engage the public in the choices and trade-offs that have to be made

New ICM research shows that 71 per cent of the public agree that 'immigration is an important topic for the public so they should have more say in how it's handled through public consultation and annual scrutiny in parliament of current immigration levels and what targets are set'.

There should be an annual migration report to Parliament, with an **annual Migration Day report** along the lines of the annual Budget, where the Home Secretary reports clearly and transparently on all migration flows, so that the House of Commons can debate the government's recommendations to maintain or amend its existing targets, and its proposals for managing migration and integration impacts.

The statistical information on migration flows and impacts should be overseen by the Migration Advisory Committee, to ensure it is robust and independent. Ministers should report on these independently-audited facts and make the government's policy recommendations.

Since we want an informed and transparent debate, it would help if the immigration figures mean what the public think they mean. That means that they should contain the people that they expect to be in them. But the current official statistical categories do not match the British public's understanding of what should count as immigration. For example, only 4 per cent of people think that British citizens returning from abroad should count as 'immigrants' for government policy. Only one in five think it makes sense for students to count as immigrants.[48] It is important to report all of these figures transparently. It is good if the government reports a fully informative range of different indicators and measures, such as immigration, the net migration of citizens and non-citizens, and so on.

But it surely assists an informed public debate if the headline immigration figures released by government, and reported on the news, do match up with what the public understand 'immigration' to mean.

There is a growing, informed consensus that questions whether international students should be included in a net migration target. The Migration Advisory Committee should be commissioned to investigate and report on the contributions and pressures associated with student migration, and its findings used to inform further discussion.

International student numbers should be reported separately in a clear and transparent way, alongside the immigration figures, with students only included in the headline immigration total if and when they remain in the UK after their studies finish. The government could choose to set a target in this specific area, which reflects its desire to increase the number of students choosing to come to the UK to study, by finding a measure to assess how the UK is maintaining its competitive position against other countries.

For asylum, it would be useful for the government to report on the previous year, and to offer forward projections and estimates of the anticipated range for future flows, linking this to its broader work on human rights, conflict prevention and development in the areas most affected. This would help to put into context the scale of current applications, currently around 20,000 a year – about one-thirtieth of UK immigration – to help to secure a cross-party consensus that asylum applications should be treated on their merits and that the UK should be actively seeking to take its fair share of those who need protection.

The annual Migration Day report to the House of Commons should provide an important hook for broader public and media discussion of immigration. The government should actively seek submissions and proposals about the overall target, or its component parts. Parliamentary committee hearings and broader public debates could scrutinise proposals and recommendations from civic society.

In the month ahead of the Migration Day debate, the government should work with local government and others to promote regional debates about the local impacts of migration – including the needs of business, the NHS and other public services, and how impacts on public services, schools and housing are being handled. The relevant Parliamentary Select Committees could report on these specific issues.

4. Giving the public the responsibility to decide about Europe

The most important immigration issue on which to engage the public is Europe. It is often said that we have no choice about EU migration. Yet that isn't quite true. It is our decision whether to stay in the European Union or not. If we choose to remain in the club, then we have to play by its rules – including those on free movement.

Given that EU membership does constrain future policy choices, it is particularly important that the public own this decision about our future. A referendum on EU membership puts this directly in the hands of the public – and so gives all citizens responsibility to decide on the trade-offs involved in being in or out of the EU.

In our view, this is a keystone to securing public ownership of the choices Britain makes about migration. The precise timing of a referendum may depend on events and reform negotiations but it is difficult to see any route to deepening public ownership of the choices Britain makes about migration politics and policy without biting this bullet.

While this is currently a position promoted by UKIP and the Conservative party, together with a minority of Liberal Democrat and Labour voices, broadening support across the party political spectrum on the case for a decisive referendum could help to ensure that the public is given a choice on this issue.

As in the Scottish referendum, the franchise should be extended to 16–17 year olds, since this vote will not just elect a government for five years but make a national decision for the next half century or more. Both sides in the referendum should embrace the challenge of putting their competing visions of Britain's future to those about to turn 18.

In our view, proposals for greater public engagement with immigration politics or policy which do not offer people a vote on this central, contested issue of EU membership are unlikely to ring true with the public.

5. Enforce employment rights and the minimum wage so British workers aren't undercut and migrant workers aren't exploited

Concerns about the impacts of immigration on jobs and wages came through strongly in deliberative research groups conducted by British Future in Bolton and Southampton to inform our 2013 report *"EU migration from Romania and Bulgaria: what does the public think?"*

ICM polling in for this report in July 2014 found that 82 per cent of people agree that 'the government must enforce the minimum wage so we have a level playing field and employers can't squeeze out British workers by employing immigrants on the cheap'.

People in lower-paid and less secure jobs, or who are seeking employment, are particularly worried that they could be shut out of the employment market by migrants who are prepared to work for less than the minimum wage or in sub-standard conditions.

Policymakers will find that both British workers and migrants alike would support measures – in effect little more than improved enforcement of existing laws – to ensure that British workers are not undercut and migrant workers are not exploited through illegally low rates of pay or poor working conditions.

6. Spread the pressures and the benefits of immigration more evenly around Britain

In the long term, perhaps the most important aspect of getting migration policy right is the distribution of migration and economic activity. There is a long-term bargain to be struck between the south-east's desire to manage pressures of population and the rest of the country's need to share in the south-east's – particularly London's – economic growth.

The Migration Day debate process should provide an opportunity for governments in Scotland and Wales to ensure there is strong civic, economic and political advocacy of the demographic needs of their countries, for the economy and public services.

The regional dimension will depend more on broader medium and long-term strategies for rebalancing economic growth than on specific migration policy measures. It is considerably more difficult politically to adopt regional migration policy measures while there is low public confidence in the competence of the immigration system.

There is limited practical scope for regionally-based immigration policy in a country the size of the United Kingdom. Certainly, the policy and political viability of such an approach depends on a level of public confidence in the management of immigration which we don't currently have.

However, while caution is advisable, there may be a case for at least exploring whether there are practical ways to meet the specific migration needs of Scotland. The SNP government in Scotland is keen to attract migration, with cross-party support. Westminster parties which are committed to the future of the United Kingdom should also be concerned to ensure Scotland's interests are not crowded out of the migration debate, particularly after the fairly close 2014 referendum result.

The Canadian points-based system may offer a model or guide for the future. It sets a different points threshold for specific provinces to encourage migrants to settle outside the economic centres of Toronto and Montreal. Given the contrasting demographic profile of Scotland and the demands of its economy for more skilled workers, the Scottish and UK governments could pilot a variation on such a system.

This might involve selected groups of migrants with specific skills needed to fill gaps in public services such as the NHS or teachers in maths, sciences and languages. Such a scheme could offer bonus points in selected skilled migration visa categories to those agreeing to live, work and stay within Scotland, or to remain with a particular employer or sector for a period of 3–5 years. Restricting the scheme initially to public sector workers would make the regular checks on the residential requirement easier to maintain. Participants would be eligible to apply for citizenship after five years, in the usual way, subject to compliance with the visa restrictions.

A pilot scheme could assess the practicality and compliance rates for such a regionalised policy. It would be in the interests of the devolved Scottish administration to put resources into monitoring and compliance, since establishing any longer-term policy would depend on showing that a pilot scheme could meet political and public concerns about compliance and enforcement.

In addition, we should ensure that better and more up-to-date monitoring establishes which towns and cities are feeling the pressures brought by immigration – on housing, school places and other public services – and ensures that resources are moved to those areas to help them cope. School rolls are a more timely way to establish where there is pressure on school places, for example, than census data.

A proposal to re-allocate EU resources, to areas where the pressures of immigration are most keenly felt, is discussed in more detail in Chapter 7, '*So what about Europe? The EU free movement conundrum*'.

7. Welfare benefits: make contribution matter and welcome contributors as club members

The public's biggest concern about the pressures of immigration concerns contribution and welfare.

It is important not to stoke anxieties, and government should commit to ensuring that public information on the levels of benefit claiming from recent migrants is made available via those independent bodies responsible increasing transparency and accountability in the immigration debate. The vast majority of migrants come here to work, and are doing so. Engaging them in a discussion, together with British citizens, about migrants' access to benefits is likely to uncover a strong consensus for sensible limits on access to benefits for new arrivals – one which some migration sceptics may find surprising.

The government should focus on regaining public trust by enforcing the limits and policies that are already in place, rather than announcing new "crackdowns" and other initiatives that only reinforce the public impression that the current system is not working.

The UK is limited in what it can do regarding access to benefits for EU citizens. It should, however, seek to stop the 'exportability' of payments such as child benefit, which can currently be paid to people not living in Britain.

This is widely seen as unfair. Most Britons will see little wrong with their hard-working neighbour from another EU country, whose kids are at the same school as theirs, receiving the same child benefit as they do. They simply will not understand why they should receive more because they have children who are not living in the UK. This situation undermines the fairness commitment that is so important to integration and majority support for immigration.

Housing is another 'pressure point' often mentioned by those expressing anxiety about the impacts of immigration. It is important that local councils exercise the powers they have available to create a system that is fair to citizens and migrants. This means social housing policies that emphasise contribution and commitment to a local area, over and against a pure 'needs-based' approach.

Having a fair and transparent allocations policy based on length of registration and prioritising those in employment will go some way to demonstrate the fairness needed to reduce tensions. Some councils – like the London Borough of Newham – have even introduced compulsory registration for social landlords in order to more effectively monitor the quality of housing in the private rented sector.

Ultimately the question of EU migrants access to benefits looks likely to only be resolved through the resolution of two much bigger questions: that of whether Britain should move to a more contribution-based, national insurance form of welfare provision; and the question of EU membership that we believe should be decided by the public in a referendum.

8. Stop immigration rules keeping British families apart
Protecting the welfare system from dependency is a legitimate public policy goal.

A pro-contribution approach should involve a review of the family marriage rules, particularly the income thresholds that oblige some Britons to leave the country in order to keep their family together.

It would also be sensible to find an appropriate formula by which the earnings of either partner could be taken into consideration. Setting the income threshold at a level where a full-time worker on the minimum wage would qualify would respect the principle of contribution better than an income threshold set at the median income level, excluding half of those in work. It should be possible for this modest reform to win broad political and public support as a pro-contribution, pro-work and pro-marriage policy, which seeks to avoid fracturing family life by splitting families up or forcing them to leave the UK.

While it is legitimate to set thresholds (based on income or skills) for incoming migrants, the core issue at stake here is about the constraints placed on existing British citizens, in their right to marry and remain in the UK, living with their husband or wife. These would be more reasonable if they did not exclude half the population.

Efforts to tackle all abuses of marriage migration routes through sham marriages should continue and be stepped up as part of any reform package, such as with current moves to strengthen the powers of registrars and their responsibilities to report concerns.

9. Make English language the keystone to integration

Being able to speak English is the key to integration and a passport to full economic, social and democratic participation in our society.

Governments should aim to achieve universal fluency in English right across the country, and work with partners to identify the most effective ways to reach those who need help to achieve proficiency in the English language.

The government should make English language lessons free at the point of use, establishing a loan scheme to pay back the cost of tuition, as David Goodhart, of the Demos thinktank, has proposed.

School pupils who arrive in the classroom without English fluency are currently enjoying strong success in the school system, particularly in London, and are contributing to a general rise of attainment levels despite this additional challenge. Greater efforts should be made to engage parents too. Health services could have an important outreach role for some of those who may not often come into contact with the state: for example, women with poor language fluency could be offered advice and support through pregnancy services and post-natal midwife care, making this as routine a practice as advice on healthy eating or information on stopping smoking, and building on the motivation of new parents to have the capacity to be involved with their children's education.

Here, the universities, who are significant beneficiaries of immigration, could be asked to contribute to achieving this goal. The Government should consult our leading universities to find practical ways to make some of their world-class facilities available – outside term-time, and at some weekends – as a practical way to assist local English language teaching projects. This could be combined with high-profile projects to actively encourage recent graduates, current students and university staff to donate time to literacy projects, for example as mentors or voluntary ESOL assistants.

This positive contribution to successful integration would be an important symbolic and practical example of how institutions that benefit culturally and economically from immigration can help the towns and cities of which they are a part to manage the challenges of making it work. It would also give citizens themselves a positive way to contribute to integration, promoting greater contact between communities. Engaging universities in how they can practically support such English language initiatives could be combined with a corresponding government commitment to support universities to actively increase enrolment of foreign students, an important source of income for universities and the local economy around them.

10. Encourage migrants to become British – and celebrate it when they do

Migrants who have been in the UK five years should be actively encouraged to take up citizenship, including EU migrants, including undertaking the language and citizenship tests.

Citizenship ceremonies offer an important way to mark the rites of passage to joining a new society. Government and local councils should work to promote citizenship ceremonies more actively, involving existing citizens more in these events as a way to welcome new Britons to our common club.

These should combine the symbolic and the practical: citizenship ceremonies should be a moment to ensure that people register to vote, and get opportunities to engage in local activities, from how to give blood to promoting civic groups.

The 800th anniversary of the Magna Carta in 2015 could be celebrated around Britain by holding citizenship ceremonies in special locations of particular local resonance, a practice that could be repeated on other high days and holidays in the national calendar.

EPILOGUE – SO, LET'S TALK ABOUT IMMIGRATION

Britain has changed a lot in our lifetimes, in many different ways. How we work, what we do outside of work and how we communicate with each other all look very different to thirty years ago. And Britain itself looks different too. The people who live here have changed a lot in that time. Some of this has happened quickly – too quickly for some. We need to find a way to manage that change in order to make it work well for all of us.

That's why we need to talk about immigration.

We can't make immigration work for Britain if we're afraid to talk openly about the challenges and pressures that rapid change can bring. That will just leave people feeling really frustrated that their concerns are dismissed and not taken seriously, while migrants who have come here will fear becoming the scapegoats for bigger problems in our economy and society.

Of course it isn't racist to worry about immigration – just as long as you talk about it without being racist.

And that's what most people want: a full, frank and fair discussion of how we can handle the challenges so that we can secure the benefits for Britain.

We should all be working together to find the solutions that can make it work fairly.

Handled well, we can benefit from immigration. It has brought us nurses and doctors who make our NHS possible. It has brought people to these shores who have built great British businesses, from M&S and Tesco to Easyjet. The food we eat, the music we listen to, the films and TV we watch and the football teams we cheer for have all been changed for the better by people who have come to Britain and contributed to our culture.

But we do need to get the balance right if we're going to make it work fairly.

So how do we make that work?

Immigration *isn't* working when the public can't have confidence in the system to know how many people are coming in or out; or when people seeking protection from war or persecution can't get a firm and fair decision quickly without being locked up or left in limbo with their lives put on hold.

"We need to invest properly in a system that's fit for purpose – that can uphold the rules in a way that is effective, fair and humane."

Immigration *isn't* working when unscrupulous employers can get away with exploiting vulnerable migrants to undercut British workers and cheat decent competitors who are playing by the rules.

Immigration *isn't* working when governments make promises they can't keep. That just undermines people's trust instead of getting them properly involved in the decisions that are right for Britain.

Those are three things that we need to change.

We need a system that people can have confidence in. To make immigration work, we need to invest properly in a system that's fit for purpose – that can uphold the rules in a way that is effective, fair and humane.

We need to be clear about what Britain expects of migrants who come here. And we also need to be clear on what we *all* need to do to make sure we have a strong and shared society, not a divided and segregated one.

And we need government to set sensible limits and to make promises they can keep – giving the public a much stronger voice in how we make the big choices about what's right for Britain.

So Britain's message to migrants should be very clear.

We have shown that you don't need to be born here to belong fully to our society but there are some things that we definitely expect.

You do need to speak our language, to obey our laws and to work hard and pay into the system.

Do that and you're welcome to be one of us: it's only fair that we treat you and your children as equally British.

But there probably are some things we are never all going to agree on. That's democracy for you. Britain's relationship with Europe, for instance. Some people think joining the European Union is the worst thing that ever happened to this country: they insist we must get out if we want control of our borders. Some think we're much better off in – and that it would damage our trading links and give us less influence to push for change if we quitted the EU and walked out.

Others aren't sure – they can see the point of being part of a big trading bloc but they don't like Europe having more sway than our own parliament and they are worried about the impact of free movement of labour – particularly when our economy is doing much better than many of our neighbours.

Whether or not we stay in the EU is a really big choice that will have a major impact on our future. We should all get a say in deciding it. Politicians should trust the people to hear all of the arguments in a referendum, make our choice, and live with the consequences.

If we chose to quit, we would need a proper real world plan so that our economy doesn't get cut off from Europe and the world. If we choose to stay in the club, then we'll have to play by its rules. If that's what we decide, then those who come here from Europe to work are playing by the rules too – and we should welcome them to Britain.

If Europe is probably the biggest issue that people disagree about, it's good that there are lots of areas where most people can agree.

We do have limits to migration. It's good to be a popular country that attracts people, but we can't take everybody who might want to come.

The right policy is to be selective – let's choose those who will contribute positively to British society, and uphold our commitments to take our fair share of those in real need of protection too.

Most people will agree that we need sensible limits: managing migration properly while keeping the skills and people we need for the success of our economy.

It's good for us all when international students choose British universities to study at, over their international competitors, bringing £7 billion a year into our economy. As long as they are genuine students, it's difficult to see why this should be mixed up with immigration.

When they graduate from British universities with useful skills that employers need, we should be glad if they want to stay on and help British firms compete in the global race – rather than taking those skills back to home to help Chinese and Indian firms compete with us.

It's good for us all if we can agree on what we need from migrants and from everyone else in society if we are going to get along together and have a Britain we can all be proud of.

So it's good for us all if we can agree on the British values we do all need to share, across every colour and creed. When integration works, the children of migrants don't see it as about 'them and us' anymore.

We must uphold freedom of religion – whether to believe or to not believe – but we shouldn't tolerate intolerance. The foundation stone is that basic British value, respect for the free speech of others – even when you don't agree with them.

We should leave the prejudices out. Old slogans like 'send them all back' belong in the past. The stereotyping of whole nationalities is wrong. Those outdated prejudices are a barrier to integration and the shared society we all need today.

From Prince Phillip and Mo Farah to the nurses and doctors who brought many of us into the world, people have shown you don't have to be born here to belong and to contribute.

But there are few benefits for Britain if we have immigration without integration.

When a country has migration without **integration**, it might be good for some migrants with a short-term goal of saving some money and it might be good for some employers too who need their labour. But it's when people integrate and become 'one of us' that Britain benefits most from migration.

Most people won't have a problem with someone who has the drive to travel across a continent to work hard and make life better for their family – as long as they make an effort to fit in and get along with their neighbours, and we have a system in place that means this can work fairly for everyone.

Immigration works when we have a system that manages the pressures but still keeps the economic benefits, and when people integrate and share our values, becoming 'one of us'. When we do this it can bring us entrepreneurs who help create jobs and growth around Britain; doctors and nurses that our NHS depends on; and even a few Olympic superstars like Mo Farah, who made us all proud to be British. So that's the fair deal we need. When migrants work hard, pay into the system, speak our language and uphold British values, they should be welcome in Britain, so that they and their children can contribute fully to our country.

Britain may be an anxious country today, but we have the best chance of all European countries at getting this right. People want an open and honest conversation about their hopes and fears over immigration and integration, identity and opportunity. It is a conversation we should have. And it can lead to a Britain that is confident, welcoming, inclusive and fair. One we can all be proud to call home.

NOTES AND TABLES

All graphics and tables are sourced from research conducted for British Future by ICM, Ipsos MORI and YouGov between November 2012 and October 2014.

Figure 1: Immigration and the economy: which of the following statements comes closest to your view?

Immigration brings both pressures and economic benefits, so we should control it and choose the immigration that's in Britain's best economic interests	Immigration is good for the economy and we should have as much as possible	Immigration is bad for the economy and we should have as little as possible
61%	7%	24%

ICM for British Future 17–19 October 2014, representative sample of 2,001 British adults aged 18 and over in GB online.

Figure 2: How much do you agree or disagree with the following statement: *"In an increasingly borderless world, we should welcome anyone who wants to come to Britain and not deter them with border controls."*

	NET: Agree	NET: Disagree	Neither
Liberals	38%	40%	22%
Anxious Middle	6%	74%	20%
Rejectionists	4%	91%	5%

ICM for British Future 17–19 October 2014, representative sample of 2,001 British adults aged 18 and over in GB online.

Figure 3: How much do you agree or disagree with the following statement: *"The government should insist that all immigrants should return to the countries they came from, whether they're here legally or illegally."*

	NET: Agree	NET: Disagree	Neither
Liberals	15%	72%	13%
Anxious Middle	18%	53%	29%
Rejectionists	66%	16%	18%

ICM for British Future 17–19 October 2014, representative sample of 2,001 British adults aged 18 and over in GB online.

Figure 4: How much do you trust the following people if or when they talk about immigration?

	David Cameron	Ed Miliband	Nick Clegg	Nigel Farage	Theresa May	Migrant of 15 years	Migrant of 15 years who became British citizen
Net: Trust	30%	27%	23%	34%	27%	51%	58%
Net: Don't Trust	59%	59%	64%	53%	54%	28%	23%

ICM for British Future 17–19 October 2014, representative sample of 2,001 British adults aged 18 and over in GB online.

Figure 5: Immigration and the economy: which of the following statements comes closest to your view (by segment).

	Immigration brings both pressures and economic benefits, so we should control it and choose the immigration that's in Britain's best economic interests	Immigration is bad for the economy and we should have as little as possible	Immigration is good for the economy and we should have as much as possible
Liberals	69	7	20
Anxious Middle	69	17	2
Rejectionists	19	79	<1

ICM for British Future 11–13 July 2014, representative sample of 2,029 British adults aged 18 and over in GB online.

Figure 6: Some migrants come to Britain to work for a few years and then return home; others make their lives here and settle in Britain. When migrants do come to Britain, which of the following options do you think is better?

	"It is better for Britain when migrants who come here put down roots and integrate into our society, becoming one of us"	"It is better for Britain when migrants come here to work for a few years without integrating and putting down roots, then returning home"
Liberals	81	19
Anxious Middle	64	36
Rejectionists	25	74

ICM for British Future 11–13 July 2014, representative sample of 2,029 British adults aged 18 and over in GB online.

Figure 7: How much do you agree or disagree with the following statement: *"Immigrants put more into Britain than they take out. Their net contribution is equivalent to more than 4p on the basic rate of income tax, worth £700 per year to someone on an average yearly wage of £26,500, according to the Organisation for Economic Co-operation and Development. This helps fund our public services, cuts the deficit and reduces the pressure for deeper cuts or higher tax rises."*

	NET: Agree	NET: Disagree	Neither
Liberals	70%	7%	23%
Anxious Middle	17%	30%	53%
Rejectionists	6%	70%	24%

ICM for British Future 11th–13th July 2014, representative sample of 2,029 British adults aged 18 and over in GB online.

Figure 8: How much do you agree or disagree with the following statement: *"Immigrants put more into Britain than they take out. Their net contribution is equivalent to more than 4p on the basic rate of income tax, worth £700 per year to someone on an average yearly wage of £26,500, according to the Organisation for Economic Co-operation and Development. This helps fund our public services, cuts the deficit and reduces the pressure for deeper cuts or higher tax rises."*

NET: Agree	NET: Disagree	Neither	Don't know
30%	30%	29%	11%

ICM for British Future 11–13 July 2014, representative sample of 2,029 British adults aged 18 and over in GB online.

Figure 9: How much do you agree or disagree with the following statement: *"Immigration can help fill gaps in the workforce: migrants do the jobs that need doing but which we struggle to fill, like care work and seasonal fruit picking. But for this to work we need to make sure standards like the minimum wage are enforced so British workers aren't undercut and migrant workers aren't exploited"*

Agree	Disagree	Neither	Don't know
65%	14%	18%	3%

ICM for British Future 11–13 July 2014, representative sample of 2,029 British adults aged 18 and over in GB online.

Figure 10: Which of the following, if any, would you say are the most important for being British?

Respect for people's right to free speech	50%
Respect for the law	46%
Speaking English	41%
Treating men and women equally	38%
Respect for all ethnic backgrounds	29%
Respect for all faiths	26%
Being born here	26%
Voting in elections	21%
Being Christian	7%
Being white	6%
Other	1%
Nothing	3%
Don't know	5%

Ipsos MORI for British Future 23–27 November 2012, representative sample of 2,515 residents of Great Britain aged 16–75.

Figure 11: How much do you agree or disagree with the following statement: *"The British war effort included Empire and Commonwealth soldiers from countries including India and the West Indies, Australia and Canada. It is important for integration today that all of our children are taught about the shared history of a multi-ethnic Britain."*

Agree	Disagree	Neither	Don't know
80%	4%	11%	6%

YouGov for British Future 9 and 10 July 2013, representative sample of 1,955 GB adults.

Figure 12: To what extent do you agree or disagree with the following statement: *"To belong to our shared society, everyone must speak our language, obey our laws and pay their taxes – so that everyone who plays by the rules counts as equally British, and should be able to reach their potential."*

Agree	Disagree	Don't know
83%	3%	14%

BritainThinks online survey for British Future 16–17 March 2013, representative sample of 2,032 adults aged 18 and over across Great Britain.

Figure 13: Some migrants come to Britain to work for a few years and then return home, others make their lives here and settle in Britain. When migrants do come to Britain, which of the following options do you think is better?

It is better for Britain when migrants who come here put down roots and integrate into our society, becoming one of us	It is better for Britain when migrants come here to work for a few years without integrating and putting down roots, then returning home
63%	37%

ICM for British Future 11–13 July 2014, representative sample of 2,029 British adults aged 18 and over in GB online.

Figure 14: Migration attitudes by party support – On a scale of 0–10, has migration had a positive or negative impact on Britain? (0 is "very negative", 10 is "very positive")

	Conservative	Labour	LibDem	UKIP
0	15	14	11	41
1	5	4	3	6
2	10	6	4	15
3	11	9	7	15
4	10	7	5	6
5	17	14	19	12
6	11	7	10	1
7	10	13	18	2
8	6	9	10	1
9	1	4	6	0
10	1	8	6	1
Don't Know	3	5	2	1

Ipsos MORI for British Future 6–11 December 2013, representative sample of 2,244 residents of Great Britain aged 16–75 online.

Figure 15: Where is the moderate majority by party?

	Liberal pro-migration (7+)	Anxious middle (2–6)	Hard line anti-migration (0–1)
UKIP	4	49	47
LibDem	40	45	14
Labour	34	43	18
Conservative	18	59	20

Ipsos MORI for British Future 6–11 December 2013, representative sample of 2,244 residents of Great Britain aged 16–75 online.

Figure 16: How much do you agree or disagree with the following statement: *"When politicians talk about immigration, I would be more likely to believe a politician who makes clear the forms of immigration we can currently control and those which we can't".*

NET: Agree	NET: Disagree	Neither	Don't know
68%	6%	17%	8%

ICM for British Future 17–19 October 2014, representative sample of 2,001 British adults aged 18 and over in GB online.

THE MODERATE MAJORITY: FURTHER POLL FINDINGS

I. How much do you agree or disagree with the following statement: *"The public should have a say in the decisions that are made about immigration. We understand that some immigration is needed for the economy and that some is outside the government's control. The government should tell us what they can do, and at what economic cost, so we can make an informed decision about what's best for Britain."*

NET: Agree	NET: Disagree	Neither	Don't know
75%	6%	13%	7%

ICM for British Future 17–19 October 2014, representative sample of 2,001 British adults aged 18 and over in GB online.

2. How much do you agree or disagree with the following statement: *"I would rather the government delivered on a realistic target to limit the immigration it can control, rather than a higher target that it may not be able to meet."*

NET: Agree	NET: Disagree	Neither	Don't know
70%	6%	16%	8%

ICM for British Future 17–19 October 2014, representative sample of 2,001 British adults aged 18 and over in GB online.

3. How much do you agree or disagree with the following statement: *"We want an immigration system that is both effective and fair, so we should invest more money in border controls."*

NET: Agree	NET: Disagree	Neither	Don't know
74%	6%	16%	4%

ICM for British Future 17–19 October 2014, representative sample of 2,001 British adults aged 18 and over in GB online.

4. How much do you agree or disagree with the following statement: *"The government must enforce the minimum wage so we have a level playing field and employers can't squeeze out British workers by employing immigrants on the cheap."*

NET: Agree	NET: Disagree	Neither	Don't know
82%	6%	9%	3%

ICM for British Future 17–19 October 2014, representative sample of 2,001 British adults aged 18 and over in GB online.

5. How much do you agree or disagree with the following statement: *"Immigration is an important topic for the public so they should have more say in how it's handled through public consultation and annual scrutiny in parliament of current immigration levels and what targets to set."*

NET: Agree	NET: Disagree	Neither	Don't know
71%	9%	17%	4%

ICM for British Future 17–19 October 2014, representative sample of 2,001 British adults aged 18 and over in GB online.

6. How much do you agree or disagree with the following statement: *"Increased immigration does have an impact on jobs, public services and the 'Britishness' of our communities. We need to manage that. But let's deal with these issues without being prejudiced and keep racism out of the debate."*

NET: Agree	NET: Disagree	Neither	Don't know
71%	9%	17%	3%

ICM for British Future 17–19 October 2014, representative sample of 2,001 British adult aged 18 and over in GB online.

7. Would you support or oppose holding a referendum on Britain's relationship with Europe within the next few years?

Support	Oppose	Don't know
57%	23%	20%

YouGov for British Future, 14–15 September 2014, representative sample of 1,703 adults aged over 18 in GB online.

8. Some politicians say they will offer an in/out referendum on Britain's membership of the EU; others have not given their support to a referendum. Which of the following do you think is the main reason for not offering an EU referendum?

Because they think the result wouldn't be the one they want	52
Because they think it would create economic uncertainty	18
Because they think referendums are a bad idea in a parliamentary democracy	9
Because they think people don't want one	2
Another reason	4
Don't know	16

YouGov for British Future, 14–15 September 2014, representative sample of 1,703 adults aged over 18 in GB online.

ABOUT BRITISH FUTURE

British Future is an independent, non-partisan thinktank engaging people's hopes and fears about integration and migration, opportunity and identity, so that we share a confident and welcoming Britain, inclusive and fair to all.

Since British Future's founding in 2012 we have conducted research on public attitudes to these issues in the UK, projecting our findings publicly to inform national debate.

Our attitudinal research has contributed to national discussions on issues including immigration from the European Union; attitudes to international students in the UK; Englishness and what it means to the English; the hopes and fears of first-time voters; and racism, discrimination and national identity in modern Britain.

We have also:

- Held events at Conservative, Labour and Lib Dem party conferences.
- Hosted a "Festival of Englishness" with IPPR to celebrate and discuss Englishness in politics, sport, literature and comedy.
- Worked with civic groups across different faiths to promote a peaceful and respectful response to the murder of corporal Lee Rigby.
- Held a "funeral for fascism" to celebrate the British public's rejection of the BNP at the ballot box and with it the demise of fascism as an electoral force in Britain.
- Launched the 'Voice of a Generation', a one-year joint project with *The Mirror* to employ a young, non-graduate apprentice reporter at the *Daily Mirror*, specifically tasked with investigating

and reporting on the most pressing concerns of young people in the run-up to the 2015 election.

• Contributed to key public debates in the national media, appearing on BBC, ITV, Channel 4 and Channel 5 TV, as well as BBC Radio and in articles in every national newspaper.

Other publications from British Future can be found online:

International Students and the UK Immigration Debate, *October 2014*

This joint report with Universities UK examines public attitudes to international students, the largest flow of non-EU migration to the UK. It finds that the public welcomes students and is 'baffled' that they are counted as migrants at all.

Voice of a Generation, *May 2014*

Commissioned for the launch of the Voice of a Generation partnership with the Daily Mirror, this report explores the most pressing concerns among 17–21 year-olds in the run-up to the 2015 general election, including on party politics, jobs, housing, debt and education.

EU migration from Romania and Bulgaria: What does the public think? *December 2013*

Based on ICM polling and workshops in Southampton, Reading and Bolton, this report examines how much people know about EU migration, their feelings towards EU migrants already here, and what they think could be done in response.

From Minority Vote to Majority Challenge, *September 2013*

An analysis of the growing importance of the ethnic minority vote in the UK, including projections as to how the 2010 election could have unfolded if the Conservative Party had secured more votes from ethnic minorities.

Do Mention the War: Will 1914 matter in 2014, *August 2013*

Released one year ahead of the First World War centenary, this report shows that many of us are unsure of what actually happened before, during and after the First World War. Yet most think it is important to seize the opportunity to learn how the First World War shaped the country we are today.

Integration Consensus 1993–2013: How Britain changed since Stephen Lawrence, *April 2013*

This report assesses how much people think the country has changed in the twenty years since Stephen Lawrence's death, showing that while racism appears to have decreased across the country, discrimination still exists.

This Sceptred Isle, *April 2012*

This report looks at what the public thinks about questions of identity, inclusion and immigration in Britain today, asking whether ethnicity or birthplace really makes a difference to being English, Scottish or Welsh.

ENDNOTES

1. Most notably Nick Lowles and Anthony Painter, *Fear and Hope, (Searchlight, February 2011); and Bobby Duffy, Perceptions and reality (Ipsos MORI, January 2014)*

2. Twenty-one per cent of people favoured current or increased levels of immigration in the annual BSA tracking poll, a proportion held steady across 2008 to 2013; British Social Attitudes 31 (2013) www.bsa-31.natcen.ac.uk/media/38108/immigration-bsa31.pdf

3. Lord Ashcroft, 'Small Island: Public opinion and the politics of immigration' (2013) www.lordashcroftpolls.com/wp-content/uploads/2013/08/LORD-ASHCROFT-Public-opinion-and-the-politics-of-immigration2.pdf

4. Searchlight, "Fear and Hope", February 2011 www.fearandhope.org.uk/executive-summary

5. For a detailed analysis of responses to economic and cultural pressure see Robert Ford and Matthew Goodwin, "Revolt on the Right" (2014)

6. Universities UK (2014), *The impact of universities on the UK economy* www.universitiesuk.ac.uk/highereducation/Pages/ImpactOfUniversities.aspx

7. Migration Observatory, University of Oxford, 'Immigration and Independence: Public Opinion on Immigration in Scotland in the Context of the Referendum Debate' (2014) www.migrationobservatory.ox.ac.uk/reports/scottish-public-opinion

8. Ian Skurnik, Carolyn Yoon, Norbert Schwartz, "Myths and facts about the flu", p.12 (University of Toronto, 2007)

9. BBC News at Ten, 26 March 2014, quoted in Katwala, 'The Clegg-Farage debate' (Open Democracy), March 2014 www.opendemocracy.net/ourkingdom/sunder-katwala/cleggfarage-debate

10. Drew Westen, 'The Political Brain The Role Of Emotion In Deciding The Fate Of The Nation' (Public Affairs, 2008) and www.thepoliticalbrain.com

11. Migrant Voice, *Migrants invisible in the media*, June 2014

12. Robert Ford Parochial and Cosmopolitan Britain: Examining the social divide in reactions to immigration, (2012) www.academia.edu/827278/Parochial_and_Cosmopolitan_Britain_Examining_the_social_divide_in_reactions_to_immigration

13. Rosamund McDougal (Optimum Population Trust, November 2006), 'What kind of population policy should the UK have?' www.populationmatters.org/documents/opt.sub.briefing.whatpoppolicy.Nov06.pdf

14. See Balanced Migration group www.balancedmigration.com

15. Press statement, Balanced Migration, May 2014 www.balancedmigration.com/2014/05/press-statement-from-the-balanced-migration-on-the-latest-immigration-statistics

16. Lord Ashcroft, "Small island: public opinion and the politics of immigration", September 2013 lordashcroftpolls.com/wp-content/uploads/2013/08/LORD-ASHCROFT-Public-opinion-and-the-politics-of-immigration2.pdf

17. Andrew Gimson, 'The Immigration Question: all agreed there were no easy answers', ConservativeHome www.conservativehome.com/thetorydiary/2014/10/the-immigration-question-all-agree-that-there-are-no-easy-answers.html

18. David Goodhart, 'Free movement in the EU need not choke us' (*Sunday Times*, 15 December 2013) www.thesundaytimes.co.uk/sto/comment/regulars/guestcolumn/article1352363.ece

19. 'Commonwealth Migrants: Memorandum by the Secretary of State for the Home Department Rab Butler', 6 October 1961, quoted in Kathleen Paul, *Whitewashing Britain*, Cornell, 1997, p. 166

20. See Sunder Katwala, "Powell more prophet than politician", March 2012 www.britishfuture.org/articles/commentary/powell-more-prophet-than-politician

21. Daniel Hannan, "The reason we can now debate immigration is that racism is in decline", *Daily Telegraph*, 8 January 2014 www.blogs.telegraph.co.uk/news/danielhannan/100253426/the-reason-we-can-now-debate-immigration-is-that-racism-is-in-decline

22. See *The integration consensus 1993-2013: How Britain changed since Stephen Lawrence, British Future, 2013* www.britishfuture.org/?s=stephen+lawrence

23. Robert Ford, Gareth Morrell and Anthony Heath, "Fewer but Better? Public Views about Immigration", British Social Attitudes Survey 29 (2012)

24. See NatCen www.natcen.ac.uk/our-research/categories/social-political-attitudes/immigration

25. For example: YouGov, "UKIP adverts are not racist", April 2014 www.yougov.co.uk/news/2014/04/24/voters-new-ukip-adverts-are-not-racist

26. "Racism and UKIP", *The Sun*, Saturday 17 May www.thesun.co.uk/sol/homepage/news/sun_says/5531814/The-Sun-says.html

27. "Ukip's New Migration Spokesman Steven Woolfe On Party's 'Ethical Immigration Policy'", 23 July 2014 www.huffingtonpost.co.uk/2014/07/23/ukip-migration-steven-woolfe_n_5613441.html

28. Douglas Carswell acceptance speech, reported on BBC news website 10 October 2014 www.bbc.co.uk/news/uk-politics-29549414

29. Rob Ford and Matthew Goodwin, "Revolt on the Right" (2014)

30. Drew Westen, 'Fear and Anxiety Around Demographic Change: Speaking Openly about the Changing Color of America' (Westen Strategies, 2014)

31. NatCen, 31st British Social Attitudes Survey, 2014 www.bsa-31.natcen.ac.uk/?_ga=1.1290201 08.1793894452.1412951026

32. British Future, "A million British Muslims reject extremists on poppy wearing", citing data from the Ethnic Minority British Election Survey (EMBES), November 2013 www. britishfuture.org/articles/news/million-british-muslims-reject-extremists-on-poppy-wearing

33. Demos, "Mapping Integration", February 2014 www.demos.co.uk/projects/mappingintegration

34. ICM for British Future, July 2014 www.britishfuture.org/blog/using-shared-first-world-war-history-teach-british-values-promote-integration

35. Eric Kaufmann and Gareth Harris: Changing Places (Demos, 2014) http://www.demos.co.uk/publications/changingplaces

36. For further discussion see IPPR, "The dog that finally barked", January 2012 www.ippr.org/publications/the-dog-that-finally-barked-england-as-an-emerging-political-community

37. YouGov (2013) reported in Matthew Goodwin, The Roots of Extremism: The English Defence League and the Counter-Jihad Challenge (Chatham House, 2013) www.chathamhouse.org/publications/papers/view/189767#sthash.gMZqUeiz.dpuf

38. Ibid.

39. Britain Thinks (2013) polling for British Future, reported in 'The Integration Consensus' (British Future, 2013)

40. Understanding Society (2012), ESRC and Institute for Social and Economic Research, University of Essex. Survey research from National Centre for Social Research. Reported in 'Muslims are truest of true Brits' (The Times, 30 June 2012) www.thetimes.co.uk/tto/news/uk/article3461486.ece

41. Transatlantic Trends (2013), German Marshall Fund

42. Jon Kelly, 'What is Baroness Warsi's dinner table test?' (BBC, 2011) www.bbc.co.uk/news/magazine-12240315

43. Heath et al: Ethnic Minority British Election Study – Key Findings (Runnymede Trust, 2012) www.runnymedetrust.org/uploads/EMBESbriefingFINALx.pdf

44. "From minority vote to majority challenge", British Future

45. Charles Clarke, 'The Too Difficult Box' (Biteback publishing, 2014)

46. David Goodhart, Independent on Sunday, 19 October 2014

47. Centre for Social Justice, 'Asylum matters – restoring trust in the UK asylum system', 2008 www.centreforsocialjustice.org.uk/publications/asylum-matters-restoring-trust-in-the-uk-asylum-system

48. British Future and Universities UK, "International Students and the UK immigration debate" (August 2014)